CREATIVE HOME BAKING

CREATIVE HOME BAKING

P A T R I C I A L O U S A D A

Dolphin Publications

This edition specially produced for
Dolphin Publications,
Bridge Mills Business Park,
Langley Road South
Pendleton
Salford, M6 6EL

First published by Dolphin Publications in 1993
and exclusive to them in the UK.

© 1993 Anness Publishing Limited
Boundary Row Studios
1 Boundary Row
London SE1 8HP

ISBN 1-873762-71-2

Editorial Director: Joanna Lorenz
Project Editor: Carole Clements
Copy Editor: Laura Washburn
Designer: Sheila Volpe
Photographer: Amanda Heywood
Food Styling: Elizabeth Wolf-Cohen, Carla Capalbo
steps by Cara Hobday, Teresa Goldfinch, Nicola Fowler

Printed and bound in Hong Kong

ACKNOWLEDGEMENTS

For their assistance in the production of this book the publishers wish to thank:

American Country Collections Limited
28 Baker Street
Weybridge, Surrey KT13 8AU

British Gas North Thames
North Thames House
London Road
Staines, Middlesex TW18 4AE

Kenwood Appliances Plc
New Lane
Havant
Hampshire PO9 2NH

M.C. Typeset Limited
The Barn, Woodbank House
Rochester Road
Wouldham, Kent ME1 3RB

Magimix
115A High Street
Godalming, Surrey GU7 1AQ

Prestige
Prestige House
22–26 High Street
Egham, Surrey TW20 9DU

CONTENTS

~

BISCUITS & BARS

~

*Keep the biscuit tin filled with this wonderful array of biscuits
and bars – some soft and chewy, some crunchy and nutty,
some rich and sinful, and some plain and wholesome.
All are irresistible.*

Farmhouse Biscuits

MAKES 18

4 oz (115 g) butter or margarine, at room
temperature

3½ oz (100 g) light brown sugar

2½ oz (70 g) crunchy peanut butter

1 egg

2 oz (55 g) plain flour

½ tsp baking powder

½ tsp ground cinnamon

⅛ tsp salt

6 oz (170 g) muesli

2 oz (55 g) raisins

2 oz (55 g) chopped walnuts

1 Preheat a 350°F/180°C/Gas 4 oven.
Grease a baking sheet.

2 With an electric mixer, cream the
butter or margarine and sugar until
light and fluffy. Beat in the peanut
butter. Beat in the egg.

3 ▲ Sift the flour, baking powder,
cinnamon and salt over the peanut
butter mixture and stir to blend. Stir
in the muesli, raisins and walnuts.
Taste the mixture to see if it needs
more sugar, as muesli varies.

4 ▲ Drop rounded tablespoonfuls of
the mixture onto the prepared baking
sheet about 1 in (2.5 cm) apart. Press
gently with the back of a spoon to
spread each mound into a circle.

5 Bake until lightly coloured, about
15 minutes. With a metal spatula,
transfer to a rack to cool. Store in
an airtight container.

Crunchy Oatmeal Biscuits

MAKES 14

6 oz (170 g) butter or margarine, at room
temperature

6 oz (170 g) caster sugar

1 egg yolk

6 oz (170 g) plain flour

1 tsp bicarbonate of soda

½ tsp salt

2 oz (55 g) rolled oats

2 oz (55 g) small crunchy nugget cereal

~ VARIATION ~

For Nutty Oatmeal Biscuits,
substitute an equal quantity of
chopped walnuts or pecans for the
cereal, and prepare as described.

1 ▲ With an electric mixer, cream
the butter or margarine and sugar
together until light and fluffy. Mix in
the egg yolk.

2 Sift over the flour, bicarbonate of
soda and salt, then stir into the butter
mixture. Add the oats and cereal and
stir to blend. Refrigerate for at least 20
minutes.

3 Preheat a 375°F/190°C/Gas 5 oven.
Grease a baking sheet.

4 ▲ Roll the mixture into balls.
Place them on the sheet and flatten
with the bottom of a floured glass.

5 Bake until golden, 10–12 minutes.
With a metal spatula, transfer to a
rack to cool completely. Store in an
airtight container.

Farmhouse Biscuits (top), Crunchy Oatmeal Biscuits

Oaty Coconut Biscuits

MAKES 48

6 oz (170 g) quick-cooking oats

3 oz (85 g) desiccated coconut

8 oz (225 g) butter or margarine, at room temperature

4 oz (115 g) caster sugar + 2 tbsp

2 oz (55 g) dark brown sugar

2 eggs

4 tbsp milk

1½ tsp vanilla essence

4 oz (115 g) plain flour

½ tsp bicarbonate of soda

½ tsp salt

1 tsp ground cinnamon

1 Preheat a 400°F/200°C/Gas 6 oven. Lightly grease 2 baking sheets.

2 ▲ Spread the oats and coconut on an ungreased baking sheet. Bake until golden brown, 8–10 minutes, stirring occasionally.

3 With an electric mixer, cream the butter or margarine and both sugars until light and fluffy. Beat in the eggs, 1 at a time, then the milk and vanilla. Sift over the dry ingredients and fold in. Stir in the oats and coconut.

4 ▼ Drop spoonfuls of the mixture 1–2 in (2.5–5 cm) apart on the prepared sheets and flatten with the bottom of a greased glass dipped in sugar. Bake until golden, 8–10 minutes. Transfer to a rack to cool.

Crunchy Jumbles

MAKES 36

4 oz (115 g) butter or margarine, at room temperature

8 oz (225 g) caster sugar

1 egg

1 tsp vanilla essence

5 oz (140 g) plain flour

½ tsp bicarbonate of soda

⅛ tsp salt

2 oz (55 g) crisped rice cereal

6 oz (170 g) chocolate chips

~ **VARIATION** ~

For even crunchier biscuits, add 2 oz (55 g) walnuts, coarsely chopped, with the cereal and chocolate chips.

1 Preheat a 350°F/180°C/Gas 4 oven. Lightly grease 2 baking sheets.

2 ▲ With an electric mixer, cream the butter or margarine and sugar until light and fluffy. Beat in the egg and vanilla. Sift over the flour, bicarbonate of soda and salt and fold in carefully.

3 ▼ Add the cereal and chocolate chips. Stir to mix thoroughly.

4 Drop spoonfuls of the mixture 1–2 in (2.5–5 cm) apart on the sheets. Bake until golden, 10–12 minutes. Transfer to a rack to cool.

Oaty Coconut Biscuits (top), Crunchy Jumbles

Cinnamon-Coated Cookies

MAKES 30

4 oz (115 g) butter, at room temperature

12 oz (350 g) caster sugar

1 tsp vanilla essence

2 eggs

2 fl oz (65 ml) milk

14 oz (400 g) plain flour

1 tsp bicarbonate of soda

2 oz (55 g) finely chopped walnuts

FOR THE COATING

5 tbsp sugar

2 tbsp ground cinnamon

1 Preheat a 375°F/190°C/Gas 5 oven. Grease 2 baking sheets.

2 With an electric mixer, cream the butter until light. Add the sugar and vanilla and continue mixing until fluffy. Beat in the eggs, then the milk.

3 ▲ Sift the flour and bicarbonate of soda over the butter mixture and stir to blend. Stir in the nuts. Refrigerate for 15 minutes.

4 ▲ For the coating, mix the sugar and cinnamon. Roll tablespoonfuls of the mixture into walnut-size balls. Roll the balls in the sugar mixture. You may need to work in batches.

5 Place 2 in (5 cm) apart on the prepared sheets and flatten slightly. Bake until golden, about 10 minutes. Transfer to a rack to cool.

Chewy Chocolate Biscuits

MAKES 18

4 egg whites

10 oz (285 g) icing sugar

4 oz (115 g) cocoa powder

2 tbsp plain flour

1 tsp instant coffee

1 tbsp water

4 oz (115 g) finely chopped walnuts

1 Preheat a 350°F/180°C/Gas 4 oven. Line 2 baking sheets with greaseproof paper and grease the paper.

~ **VARIATION** ~

If wished, add 3 oz (85 g) chocolate chips to the mixture with the nuts.

2 With an electric mixer, beat the egg whites until frothy.

3 ▼ Sift the sugar, cocoa, flour and coffee into the whites. Add the water and continue beating on low speed to blend, then on high for a few minutes until the mixture thickens. With a rubber spatula, fold in the walnuts.

4 ▲ Place generous spoonfuls of the mixture 1 in (2.5 cm) apart on the prepared sheets. Bake until firm and cracked on top but soft on the inside, 12–15 minutes. With a metal spatula, transfer to a rack to cool.

Cinnamon-Coated Cookies (top), Chewy Chocolate Biscuits

Ginger Biscuits

MAKES 36

8 oz (225 g) caster sugar

3½ oz (100 g) light brown sugar

4 oz (115 g) butter, at room temperature

4 oz (115 g) margarine, at room temperature

1 egg

3 fl oz (85 ml) black treacle

9 oz (250 g) plain flour

2 tsp ground ginger

½ tsp grated nutmeg

1 tsp ground cinnamon

2 tsp bicarbonate of soda

½ tsp salt

1 Preheat a 325°F/170°F/Gas 3 oven. Line 2–3 baking sheets with greaseproof paper and grease lightly.

2 ▲ With an electric mixer, cream half of the caster sugar, the brown sugar, butter and margarine until light and fluffy. Add the egg and continue beating to blend well. Add the treacle.

3 ▲ Sift the dry ingredients 3 times, then stir into the butter mixture. Refrigerate for 30 minutes.

4 ▲ Place the remaining sugar in a shallow dish. Roll tablespoonfuls of the biscuit mixture into balls, then roll the balls in the sugar to coat.

5 Place the balls 2 in (5 cm) apart on the prepared sheets and flatten slightly. Bake until golden around the edges but soft in the middle, 12–15 minutes. Let stand for 5 minutes before transferring to a rack to cool.

~ **VARIATION** ~

To make Gingerbread Men, increase the amount of flour by 1 oz (30 g). Roll out the mixture and cut out shapes with a special cutter. Decorate with icing, if wished.

Cream Cheese Spirals

MAKES 32

8 oz (225 g) butter, at room temperature
8 oz (225 g) cream cheese
2 tsp caster sugar
8 oz (225 g) plain flour
1 egg white beaten with 1 tbsp water, for glazing
caster sugar, for sprinkling
FOR THE FILLING
4 oz (115 g) finely chopped walnuts
4 oz (115 g) light brown sugar
1 tsp ground cinnamon

1 With an electric mixer, cream the butter, cream cheese and sugar until soft. Sift over the flour and mix until combined. Gather into a ball and divide in half. Flatten each half, wrap in greaseproof paper and refrigerate for at least 30 minutes.

2 Meanwhile, make the filling. Mix together the chopped walnuts, the brown sugar and the cinnamon. Set aside.

3 Preheat a 375°F/190°F/Gas 5 oven. Grease 2 baking sheets.

4 ▲ Working with one half of the mixture at a time, roll out thinly into a circle about 11 in (28 cm) in diameter. Trim the edges with a knife, using a dinner plate as a guide.

5 ▼ Brush the surface with the egg white glaze and then sprinkle evenly with half the filling.

6 Cut the circle into quarters, and each quarter into 4 sections, to form 16 triangles.

7 ▲ Starting from the base of the triangles, roll up to form spirals.

8 Place on the sheets and brush with the remaining glaze. Sprinkle with caster sugar. Bake until golden, 15–20 minutes. Cool on a rack.

Raspberry Sandwich Biscuits

Makes 32

6 oz (170 g) blanched almonds

6 oz (170 g) plain flour

6 oz (170 g) butter, at room temperature

4 oz (115 g) caster sugar

grated rind of 1 lemon

1 tsp vanilla essence

1 egg white

⅛ tsp salt

1 oz (30 g) flaked almonds

8 fl oz (250 ml) raspberry jam

1 tbsp fresh lemon juice

1 Place the blanched almonds and 3 tablespoons of the flour in a food processor, blender or grinder and process until finely ground. Set aside.

2 With an electric mixer, cream the butter and sugar together until light and fluffy. Stir in the lemon rind and vanilla. Add the ground almonds and remaining flour and mix well until combined. Gather into a ball, wrap in greaseproof paper, and refrigerate for at least 1 hour.

3 Preheat a 325°F/170°C/Gas 3 oven. Line 2 baking sheets with greaseproof paper.

4 Divide the biscuit mixture into 4 equal parts. Working with one section at a time, roll out to a thickness of ⅛ in (3 mm) on a lightly floured surface. With a 2½ in (6 cm) fluted pastry cutter, stamp out circles. Gather the scraps, roll out and stamp out more circles. Repeat with the remaining sections.

5 ▲ Using a ¾ in (2 cm) piping nozzle or pastry cutter, stamp out the centres from half the circles. Place the rings and circles 1 in (2.5 cm) apart on the prepared sheets.

6 ▲ Whisk the egg white with the salt until just frothy. Chop the flaked almonds. Brush only the biscuit rings with the egg white, then sprinkle over the almonds. Bake until very lightly browned, 12–15 minutes. Let cool for a few minutes on the sheets before transferring to a rack.

7 ▲ In a saucepan, melt the jam with the lemon juice until it comes to a simmer. Brush the jam over the biscuit circles and sandwich together with the rings. Store in an airtight container with sheets of greaseproof paper between the layers.

Christmas Cookies

MAKES 30

6 oz (170 g) unsalted butter, at room
temperature

10 oz (285 g) caster sugar

1 egg

1 egg yolk

1 tsp vanilla essence

grated rind of 1 lemon

¼ tsp salt

10 oz (285 g) plain flour

FOR DECORATING (OPTIONAL)

coloured icing and small decorations

1 Preheat a 350°F/180°C/Gas 4 oven.

2 ▲ With an electric mixer, cream
the butter until soft. Add the sugar
gradually and continue beating until
light and fluffy.

3 ▲ Using a wooden spoon, slowly
mix in the whole egg and the egg yolk.
Add the vanilla, lemon rind and salt.
Stir to mix well.

4 Add the flour and stir until
blended. Gather the mixture into a
ball, wrap in greaseproof paper, and
refrigerate for at least 30 minutes.

5 ▼ On a floured surface, roll out the
mixture about ⅛ in (3 mm) thick.

6 ▲ Stamp out shapes or rounds with
biscuit cutters.

7 Bake until lightly coloured, about 8
minutes. Transfer to a rack and let
cool completely before icing and
decorating, if wished.

Toasted Oat Meringues

MAKES 12

2 oz (55 g) rolled oats
2 egg whites
⅛ tsp salt
1½ tsp cornflour
6 oz (170 g) caster sugar

1 Preheat a 275°F/140°C/Gas 1 oven. Spread the oats on a baking sheet and toast in the oven until golden, about 10 minutes. Lower the heat to 250°F/130°C/Gas ½. Grease and flour a baking sheet.

> ### ~ VARIATION ~
>
> Add ½ teaspoon ground cinnamon with the oats, and fold in gently.

2 ▼ With an electric mixer, beat the egg whites and salt until they start to form soft peaks.

3 Sift over the cornflour and continue beating until the whites hold stiff peaks. Add half the sugar and whisk until glossy.

4 ▲ Add the remaining sugar and fold in, then fold in the oats.

5 Gently spoon the mixture onto the prepared sheet and bake for 2 hours.

6 When done, turn off the oven. Lift the meringues from the sheet, turn over, and set in another place on the sheet to prevent sticking. Leave in the oven as it cools down.

Meringues

MAKES 24

4 egg whites
⅛ tsp salt
10 oz (285 g) caster sugar
½ tsp vanilla or almond essence (optional)
8 fl oz (250 ml) whipped cream (optional)

1 Preheat a 225°F/110°C/Gas ¼ oven. Grease and flour 2 large baking sheets.

2 With an electric mixer, beat the egg whites and salt in a very clean metal bowl on low speed. When they start to form soft peaks, add half the sugar and continue beating until the mixture holds stiff peaks.

3 ▲ With a large metal spoon, fold in the remaining sugar and vanilla or almond essence, if using.

4 ▼ Pipe the meringue mixture or gently spoon it on the prepared sheet.

5 Bake for 2 hours. Turn off the oven. Loosen the meringues, invert, and set in another place on the sheets to prevent sticking. Leave in the oven as it cools. Serve sandwiched with whipped cream, if wished.

Toasted Oat Meringues (top), Meringues

Chocolate Macaroons

MAKES 24

2 oz (55 g) plain chocolate
6 oz (170 g) blanched almonds
8 oz (225 g) caster sugar
3 egg whites
½ tsp vanilla essence
¼ tsp almond essence
icing sugar, for dusting

1 Preheat a 325°F/170°C/Gas 3 oven. Line 2 baking sheets with greaseproof paper and grease the paper.

2 ▼ Melt the chocolate in the top of a double boiler, or in a heatproof bowl set over a pan of hot water.

3 ▲ Grind the almonds finely in a food processor, blender or grinder. Transfer to a mixing bowl.

4 ▲ Add the sugar, egg whites, vanilla, and almond essence and stir to blend. Stir in the chocolate. The mixture should just hold its shape. If it is too soft, refrigerate for 15 minutes.

5 ▲ Use a teaspoon and your hands to shape the mixture into walnut-size balls. Place on the sheets and flatten slightly. Brush each ball with a little water and sift over a thin layer of icing sugar. Bake until just firm, 10–12 minutes. With a metal spatula, transfer to a rack to cool.

~ VARIATION ~

For Chocolate Pine Nut Macaroons, spread 3 oz (85 g) pine nuts in a shallow dish. Press the chocolate macaroon balls into the nuts to cover one side and bake as described, nut-side up.

Coconut Macaroons

MAKES 24

1½ oz (45 g) plain flour
⅛ tsp salt
8 oz (225 g) desiccated coconut
5½ fl oz (170 ml) sweetened condensed milk
1 tsp vanilla essence

1 Preheat a 350°F/180°C/Gas 4 oven. Grease 2 baking sheets.

2 Sift the flour and salt into a bowl. Stir in the coconut.

3 ▲ Pour in the milk. Add the vanilla and stir from the centre to make a very thick mixture.

4 ▼ Drop heaped tablespoonfuls of mixture 1 in (2.5 cm) apart on the sheets. Bake until golden brown, about 20 minutes. Cool on a rack.

Chocolate Macaroons (top), Coconut Macaroons

Shortbread

MAKES 8

5 oz (140 g) unsalted butter, at room temperature

4 oz (115 g) caster sugar

5 oz (140 g) plain flour

2½ oz (70 g) rice flour

¼ tsp baking powder

⅛ tsp salt

1 Preheat a 325°F/170°C/Gas 3 oven. Grease a shallow 8 in (20 cm) cake tin.

2 With an electric mixer, cream the butter and sugar together until light and fluffy. Sift over the flours, baking powder and salt and mix well.

3 ▲ Press the mixture neatly into the prepared tin, smoothing the surface with the back of a spoon.

4 Prick all over with a fork, then score into 8 equal wedges.

5 ▲ Bake until golden, 40–45 minutes. Leave in the tin until cool enough to handle, then unmould and recut the wedges while still hot. Store in an airtight container.

Flapjacks

MAKES 8

2 oz (55 g) butter

1 rounded tbsp golden syrup

2½ oz (70 g) dark brown sugar

4 oz (115 g) quick-cooking oats

⅛ tsp salt

1 ▲ Preheat a 350°F/180°C/Gas 4 oven. Line and grease an 8 in (20 cm) shallow cake tin.

2 ▼ Place the butter, golden syrup and sugar in a pan over low heat. Cook, stirring, until melted and combined.

~ **VARIATION** ~

If wished, add 1 teaspoon ground ginger to the melted butter.

3 ▲ Remove from the heat and add the oats and salt. Stir to blend.

4 Spoon into the prepared tin and smooth the surface. Place in the centre of the oven and bake until golden brown, 20–25 minutes. Leave in the tin until cool enough to handle, then unmould and cut into wedges while still hot.

Shortbread (top), Flapjacks

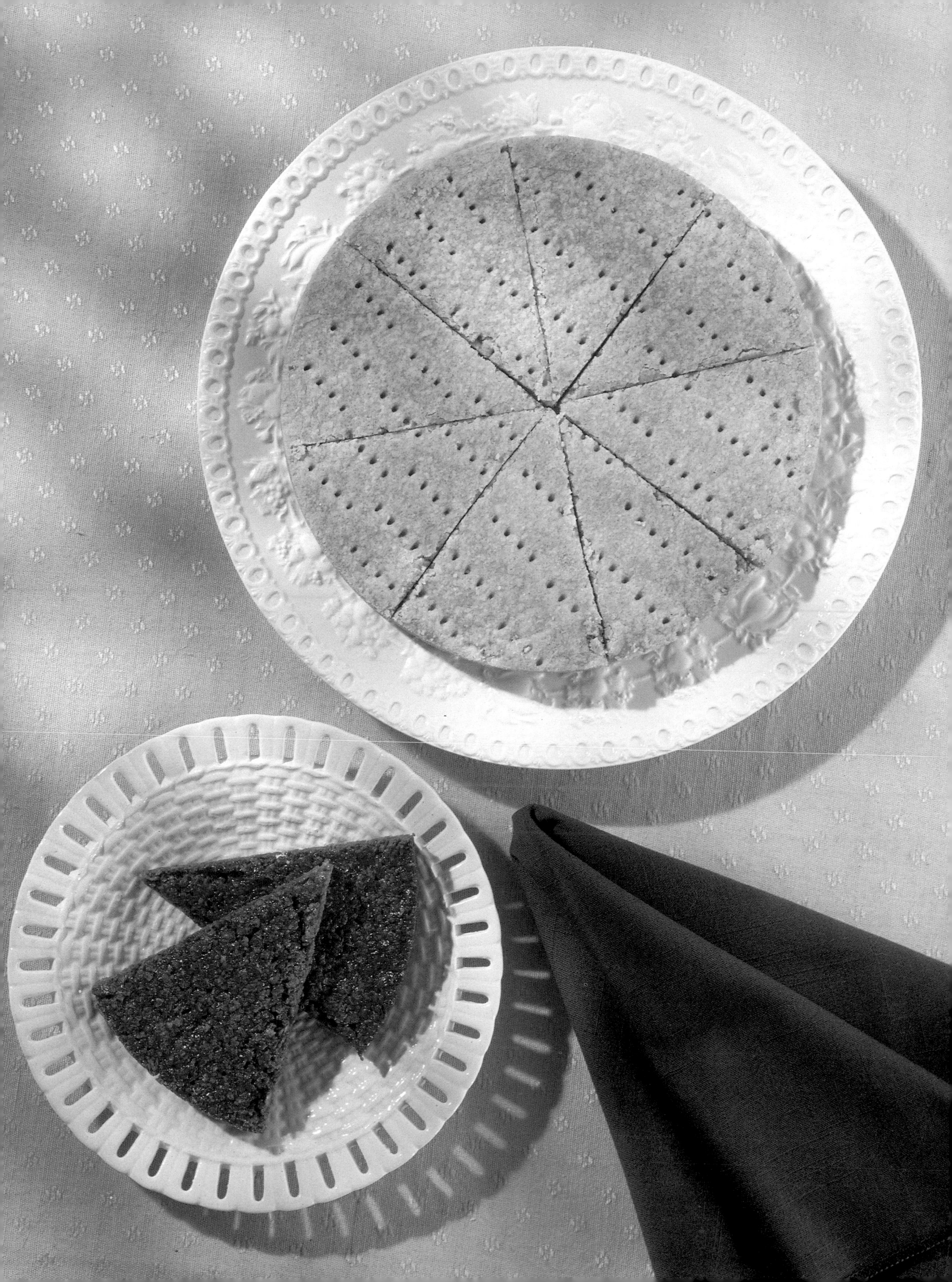

Chocolate Delights

MAKES 50

1 oz (30 g) plain chocolate
1 oz (30 g) bitter cooking chocolate
8 oz (225 g) plain flour
½ tsp salt
8 oz (225 g) unsalted butter, at room temperature
8 oz (225 g) caster sugar
2 eggs
1 tsp vanilla essence
4 oz (115 g) finely chopped walnuts

1 Melt the chocolates in the top of a double boiler, or in a heatproof bowl set over a pan of gently simmering water. Set aside.

2 ▼ In a small bowl, sift together the flour and salt. Set aside.

3 With an electric mixer, cream the butter until soft. Add the sugar and continue beating until the mixture is light and fluffy.

4 Mix the eggs and vanilla, then gradually stir into the butter mixture.

5 ▲ Stir in the chocolate, then the flour. Stir in the nuts.

6 ▲ Divide the mixture into 4 equal parts, and roll each into 2 in (5 cm) diameter logs. Wrap tightly in foil and refrigerate or freeze until firm.

7 Preheat a 375°F/190°C/Gas 5 oven. Grease 2 baking sheets.

8 With a sharp knife, cut the logs into ¼ in (5 mm) slices. Place the rounds on the prepared sheets and bake until lightly coloured, about 10 minutes. Transfer to a rack to cool.

~ **VARIATION** ~

For two-tone biscuits, melt only half the chocolate. Combine all the ingredients, except the chocolate, as above. Divide the mixture in half. Add the chocolate to one half. Roll out the plain mixture to a flat sheet. Roll out the chocolate mixture, place on top of the plain one and roll up. Wrap, slice and bake as described.

Cinnamon Treats

MAKES 50

9 oz (250 g) plain flour
½ tsp salt
2 tsp ground cinnamon
8 oz (225 g) unsalted butter, at room temperature
8 oz (225 g) caster sugar
2 eggs
1 tsp vanilla essence

1 In a bowl, sift together the flour, salt and cinnamon. Set aside.

2 ▲ With an electric mixer, cream the butter until soft. Add the sugar and continue beating until the mixture is light and fluffy.

3 Beat the eggs and vanilla, then gradually stir into the butter mixture.

4 ▲ Stir in the dry ingredients.

5 ▲ Divide the mixture into 4 equal parts, then roll each into 2 in (5 cm) diameter logs. Wrap tightly in foil and refrigerate or freeze until firm.

6 Preheat a 375°F/190°C/Gas 5 oven. Grease 2 baking sheets.

7 ▼ With a sharp knife, cut the logs into ¼ in (5 mm) slices. Place the rounds on the prepared sheets and bake until lightly coloured, about 10 minutes. With a metal spatula, transfer to a rack to cool.

Nutty Chocolate Squares

MAKES 16

2 eggs

2 tsp vanilla essence

⅛ tsp salt

6 oz (170 g) pecan nuts, coarsely chopped

2 oz (55 g) plain flour

2 oz (55 g) caster sugar

4 fl oz (125 ml) golden syrup

3 oz (85 g) plain chocolate, finely chopped

1½ oz (45 g) butter

16 pecan halves, for decorating

1 Preheat a 325°F/170°C/Gas 3 oven. Line the bottom and sides of an 8 in (20 cm) square baking tin with greaseproof paper and grease lightly.

2 ▼ Whisk together the eggs, vanilla and salt. In another bowl, mix together the pecans and flour. Set both aside.

3 In a saucepan, bring the sugar and golden syrup to a boil. Remove from the heat and stir in the chocolate and butter and blend thoroughly with a wooden spoon.

4 ▲ Mix in the beaten eggs, then fold in the pecan mixture.

5 Pour the mixture into the prepared tin and bake until set, about 35 minutes. Cool in the tin for 10 minutes before unmoulding. Cut into 2 in (5 cm) squares and press pecan halves into the tops while warm. Cool completely on a rack.

Raisin Brownies

MAKES 16

4 oz (115 g) butter or margarine

2 oz (55 g) cocoa powder

2 eggs

8 oz (225 g) caster sugar

1 tsp vanilla essence

1½ oz (45 g) plain flour

3 oz (85 g) chopped walnuts

3 oz (85 g) raisins

1 Preheat a 350°F/180°C/Gas 4 oven. Line the bottom and sides of an 8 in (20 cm) square baking tin with greaseproof paper and grease the paper.

2 ▼ Gently melt the butter or margarine in a small saucepan. Remove from the heat and stir in the cocoa powder.

3 With an electric mixer, beat the eggs, sugar and vanilla together until light. Add the cocoa mixture and stir to blend.

4 ▲ Sift the flour over the cocoa mixture and gently fold in. Add the walnuts and raisins and scrape the mixture into the prepared tin.

5 Bake in the centre of the oven for 30 minutes. Do not overbake. Leave in the tin to cool before cutting into 2 in (5 cm) squares and removing. The brownies should be soft and moist.

Nutty Chocolate Squares (top), Raisin Brownies

Figgy Bars

MAKES 48

12 oz (350 g) dried figs
3 eggs
6 oz (170 g) caster sugar
3 oz (85 g) plain flour
1 tsp baking powder
½ tsp ground cinnamon
¼ tsp ground cloves
¼ tsp grated nutmeg
¼ tsp salt
3 oz (85 g) finely chopped walnuts
2 tbsp brandy or cognac
icing sugar, for dusting

1 Preheat a 325°F/170°C/Gas 3 oven.

2 Line a 12 × 8 × 1½ in (30 × 20 × 3 cm) tin with greaseproof paper and grease the paper.

3 ▲ With a sharp knife, chop the figs roughly. Set aside.

4 In a bowl, whisk the eggs and sugar until well blended. In another bowl, sift together the dry ingredients, then fold into the egg mixture in several batches.

5 ▼ Stir in the figs, walnuts and brandy or cognac.

6 Scrape the mixture into the prepared tin and bake until the top is firm and brown, 35–40 minutes. It should still be soft underneath.

7 Let cool in the tin for 5 minutes, then unmould and transfer to a sheet of greaseproof paper lightly sprinkled with icing sugar. Cut into bars.

Lemon Bars

MAKES 36

2 oz (55 g) icing sugar
6 oz (170 g) plain flour
½ tsp salt
6 oz (170 g) butter, cut in small pieces
FOR THE TOPPING
4 eggs
12 oz (350 g) caster sugar
grated rind of 1 lemon
4 fl oz (125 ml) fresh lemon juice
6 fl oz (175 ml) whipping cream
icing sugar, for dusting

1 Preheat a 325°F/170°C/Gas 3 oven.

2 Grease a 13 × 9 in (33 × 23 cm) baking tin.

3 Sift the sugar, flour and salt into a bowl. With a pastry blender, cut in the butter until the mixture resembles coarse breadcrumbs.

4 ▲ Press the mixture into the bottom of the prepared tin. Bake until golden brown, about 20 minutes.

5 Meanwhile, for the topping, whisk the eggs and sugar together until blended. Add the lemon rind and juice and mix well.

6 ▲ Lightly whip the cream and fold into the egg mixture. Pour over the still warm base, return to the oven, and bake until set, about 40 minutes.

7 Cool completely before cutting into bars. Dust with icing sugar.

Figgy Bars (top), Lemon Bars

Apricot Specials

MAKES 12

3½ oz (100 g) light brown sugar

3 oz (85 g) plain flour

3 oz (85 g) cold unsalted butter, cut in pieces

FOR THE TOPPING

5 oz (140 g) dried apricots

8 fl oz (250 ml) water

grated rind of 1 lemon

2½ oz (75 g) caster sugar

2 tsp cornflour

2 oz (55 g) chopped walnuts

1 Preheat a 350°F/180°C/Gas 4 oven.

2 ▲ In a bowl, combine the brown sugar and flour. With a pastry blender, cut in the butter until the mixture resembles coarse breadcrumbs.

3 ▲ Transfer to an 8 in (20 cm) square baking tin and press level. Bake for 15 minutes. Remove from the oven but leave the oven on.

4 Meanwhile, for the topping, combine the apricots and water in a saucepan and simmer until soft, about 10 minutes. Strain the liquid and reserve. Chop the apricots.

5 ▲ Return the apricots to the saucepan and add the lemon rind, caster sugar, cornflour, and 4 tablespoons of the soaking liquid. Cook for 1 minute.

6 ▲ Cool slightly before spreading the topping over the base. Sprinkle over the walnuts and continue baking for 20 minutes more. Let cool in the tin before cutting into bars.

Brandysnaps

MAKES 18

2 oz (55 g) butter, at room temperature
5 oz (140 g) caster sugar
1 rounded tbsp golden syrup
1½ oz (45 g) plain flour
½ tsp ground ginger
FOR THE FILLING
8 fl oz (250 ml) whipping cream
2 tbsp brandy

1 With an electric mixer, cream together the butter and sugar until light and fluffy, then beat in the golden syrup. Sift over the flour and ginger and mix together.

2 ▲ Transfer the mixture to a work surface and knead until smooth. Cover and refrigerate for 30 minutes.

3 Preheat a 375°F/190°C/Gas 5 oven. Grease a baking sheet.

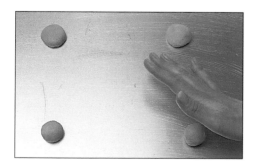

4 ▲ Working in batches of 4, form the mixture into walnut-size balls. Place far apart on the sheet and flatten slightly. Bake until golden and bubbling, about 10 minutes.

5 ▼ Remove from the oven and let cool a few moments. Working quickly, slide a metal spatula under each one, turn over, and wrap around the handle of a wooden spoon (have 4 spoons ready). If they firm up too quickly, reheat for a few seconds to soften. When firm, slide the snaps off and place on a rack to cool.

6 ▲ When all the brandy snaps are cool, prepare the filling. Whip the cream and brandy until soft peaks form. Fill a piping bag with the brandy cream. Pipe into each end of the brandy snaps just before serving.

BUNS & TEA BREADS

~

*Easy to make and satisfying to eat, these buns and tea breads
will fill the house with mouthwatering scents and lure your
family and friends to linger over breakfast, coffee or tea —
and they are great for snacks or lunch.*

Chocolate Chip Buns

MAKES 10

4 oz (115 g) butter or margarine, at room temperature

2½ oz (75 g) caster sugar

2 tbsp dark brown sugar

2 eggs, at room temperature

6 oz (170 g) plain flour

1 tsp baking powder

4 fl oz (125 ml) milk

6 oz (170 g) plain chocolate chips

1 Preheat a 375°F/190°C/Gas 5 oven. Grease 10 cups of a bun tray or use paper cases.

2 ▼ With an electric mixer, cream the butter until soft. Add both sugars and continue beating until light and fluffy. Beat in the eggs, 1 at a time.

3 Sift together the flour and baking powder, twice. Fold into the butter mixture, alternating with the milk.

4 ▲ Divide half the mixture between the greased cups. Sprinkle several chocolate chips on top, then cover with a spoonful of the mixture. To ensure even baking, half-fill any empty cups with water.

5 Bake until lightly coloured, about 25 minutes. Let stand 5 minutes before unmoulding.

Chocolate Walnut Buns

MAKES 12

6 oz (170 g) unsalted butter

4 oz (115 g) plain chocolate

1 oz (30 g) bitter cooking chocolate

8 oz (225 g) caster sugar

1¾ oz (50 g) dark brown sugar

4 eggs

1 tsp vanilla essence

¼ tsp almond essence

3 oz (85 g) plain flour

4 oz (115 g) chopped walnuts

1 Preheat a 350°F/180°C/Gas 4 oven. Grease a 12-cup bun tray or use paper cases.

2 ▼ Melt the butter with the chocolates in the top of a double boiler or in a heatproof bowl set over a pan of hot water. Transfer to a large mixing bowl.

3 Stir both the sugars into the chocolate mixture. Mix in the eggs, 1 at a time, then add the vanilla and almond essence.

4 Sift over the flour and fold in.

5 ▲ Stir in the walnuts.

6 Fill the greased cups almost to the top and bake until a skewer inserted in the centre barely comes out clean, 30–35 minutes. Let stand 5 minutes before transferring to a rack to cool completely.

Chocolate Chip Buns (top), Chocolate Walnut Buns

Raisin Bran Buns

MAKES 15

2 oz (55 g) butter or margarine
1½ oz (45 g) plain flour
2 oz (55 g) wholewheat flour
1½ tsp bicarbonate of soda
⅛ tsp salt
1 tsp ground cinnamon
1 oz (30 g) bran
3 oz (85 g) raisins
2½ oz (65 g) dark brown sugar
2 oz (55 g) caster sugar
1 egg
8 fl oz (250 ml) buttermilk
juice of ½ lemon

1 Preheat a 400°F/200°C/Gas 6 oven. Grease 15 bun-tray cups.

2 ▲ Place the butter or margarine in a saucepan and melt over gentle heat. Set aside.

3 In a mixing bowl, sift together the flours, bicarbonate of soda, salt and cinnamon.

4 ▲ Add the bran, raisins and sugars and stir until blended.

5 In another bowl, mix together the egg, buttermilk, lemon juice and melted butter.

6 ▲ Add the buttermilk mixture to the dry ingredients and stir lightly and quickly just until moistened; do not mix until smooth.

7 ▲ Spoon the mixture into the prepared bun tray, filling the cups almost to the top. Half-fill any empty cups with water.

8 Bake until golden, 15–20 minutes. Serve warm or at room temperature.

Raspberry Crumble Buns

MAKES 12

6 oz (170 g) plain flour

2 oz (55 g) caster sugar

1¾ oz (50 g) light brown sugar

2 tsp baking powder

⅛ tsp salt

1 tsp ground cinnamon

4 oz (115 g) butter, melted

1 egg

4 fl oz (125 ml) milk

5 oz (140 g) fresh raspberries

grated rind of 1 lemon

FOR THE CRUMBLE TOPPING

1 oz (30 g) finely chopped pecan nuts or walnuts

2 oz (55 g) dark brown sugar

3 tbsp plain flour

1 tsp ground cinnamon

3 tbsp butter, melted

1 Preheat a 350°F/180°C/Gas 4 oven. Grease a 12-cup bun tray or use paper cases.

2 Sift the flour into a bowl. Add the sugars, baking powder, salt and cinnamon and stir to blend.

3 ▲ Make a well in the centre. Place the butter, egg and milk in the well and mix until just combined. Stir in the raspberries and lemon rind. Spoon the mixture into the prepared bun tray, filling the cups almost to the top.

4 ▼ For the crumble topping, mix the nuts, dark brown sugar, flour and cinnamon in a bowl. Add the melted butter and stir to blend.

5 ▲ Spoon some of the crumble over each bun. Bake until browned, about 25 minutes. Transfer to a rack to cool slightly. Serve warm.

Carrot Buns

MAKES 12

6 oz (170 g) margarine, at room
temperature

3½ oz (100 g) dark brown sugar

1 egg, at room temperature

1 tbsp water

8 oz (225 g) carrots, grated

5 oz (140 g) plain flour

1 tsp baking powder

½ tsp bicarbonate of soda

1 tsp ground cinnamon

¼ tsp grated nutmeg

½ tsp salt

1 Preheat a 350°F/180°C/Gas 4 oven.
Grease a 12-cup bun tray or use paper
cases.

2 With an electric mixer, cream the
margarine and sugar until light and
fluffy. Beat in the egg and water.

3 ▲ Stir in the carrots.

4 Sift over the flour, baking powder,
bicarbonate of soda, cinnamon,
nutmeg and salt. Stir to blend.

5 ▼ Spoon the mixture into the
prepared bun tray, filling the cups
almost to the top. Bake until the tops
spring back when touched lightly,
about 35 minutes. Let stand 10
minutes before transferring to a rack.

Dried Cherry Buns

MAKES 16

8 fl oz (250 ml) plain yoghurt

6 oz (170 g) dried cherries

4 oz (115 g) butter, at room temperature

6 oz (170 g) caster sugar

2 eggs, at room temperature

1 tsp vanilla essence

7 oz (200 g) plain flour

2 tsp baking powder

1 tsp bicarbonate of soda

⅛ tsp salt

1 In a mixing bowl, combine the
yoghurt and cherries. Cover and let
stand for 30 minutes.

2 Preheat a 350°F/180°C/Gas 4 oven.
Grease 16 bun-tray cups or use paper
cases.

3 With an electric mixer, cream the
butter and sugar together until light
and fluffy.

4 ▼ Add the eggs, 1 at a time,
beating well after each addition. Add
the vanilla and the cherry mixture and
stir to blend. Set aside.

5 ▲ In another bowl, sift together
the flour, baking powder, bicarbonate
soda and salt. Fold into the cherry
mixture in 3 batches.

6 Fill the prepared cups two-thirds
full. For even baking, half-fill any
empty cups with water. Bake until the
tops spring back when touched
lightly, about 20 minutes. Transfer to
a rack to cool.

Carrot Buns (top), Dried Cherry Buns

Fruity Tea Bread

MAKES 1 LOAF

8 oz (225 g) plain flour

4 oz (115 g) caster sugar

1 tbsp baking powder

½ tsp salt

grated rind of 1 large orange

5½ fl oz (170 ml) fresh orange juice

2 eggs, lightly beaten

3 oz (85 g) butter or margarine, melted

4 oz (115 g) fresh cranberries, or bilberries

2 oz (55 g) chopped walnuts

1 Preheat a 350°F/180°C/Gas 4 oven. Line a 9 × 5 in (23 × 13 cm) loaf tin with greaseproof paper and grease.

2 Sift the flour, sugar, baking powder and salt into a mixing bowl.

3 ▼ Stir in the orange rind.

4 ▲ Make a well in the centre and add the orange juice, eggs and melted butter or margarine. Stir from the centre until the ingredients are blended; do not overmix.

5 ▲ Add the berries and walnuts and stir until blended.

6 Transfer the mixture to the prepared tin and bake until a skewer inserted in the centre comes out clean, 45–50 minutes.

7 ▲ Let cool in the tin for 10 minutes before transferring to a rack to cool completely. Serve thinly sliced, toasted or plain, with butter or cream cheese and jam.

Date and Pecan Loaf

MAKES 1 LOAF

6 oz (170 g) stoned dates, chopped
6 fl oz (175 ml) boiling water
2 oz (55 g) unsalted butter, at room temperature
2 oz (55 g) dark brown sugar
2 oz (55 g) caster sugar
1 egg, at room temperature
2 tbsp brandy
5½ oz (165 g) plain flour
2 tsp baking powder
½ tsp salt
¾ tsp freshly grated nutmeg
3 oz (85 g) coarsely chopped pecans or walnuts

1 ▲ Place the dates in a bowl and pour over the boiling water. Set aside to cool.

2 Preheat a 350°F/180°C/Gas 4 oven. Line a 9 × 5 in (23 × 13 cm) loaf tin with greaseproof paper and grease.

3 ▲ With an electric mixer, cream the butter and sugars until light and fluffy. Beat in the egg and brandy, then set aside.

4 Sift the flour, baking powder, salt and nutmeg together, 3 times.

5 ▼ Fold the dry ingredients into the sugar mixture in 3 batches, alternating with the dates and water.

6 ▲ Fold in the nuts.

7 Pour the mixture into the prepared tin and bake until a skewer inserted in the centre comes out clean, 45--50 minutes. Let cool in the tin for 10 minutes before transferring to a rack to cool completely.

Wholewheat Banana Nut Loaf

MAKES 1 LOAF

4 oz (115 g) butter, at room temperature

4 oz (115 g) caster sugar

2 eggs, at room temperature

4 oz (115 g) plain flour

1 tsp bicarbonate of soda

¼ tsp salt

1 tsp ground cinnamon

2 oz (55 g) wholewheat flour

3 large ripe bananas

1 tsp vanilla essence

2 oz (55 g) chopped walnuts

1 Preheat a 350°F/180°C/Gas 4 oven. Line the bottom and sides of a 9 × 5 in (23 × 13 cm) loaf tin with greaseproof paper and grease the paper.

2 With an electric mixer, cream the butter and sugar together until light and fluffy.

3 ▲ Add the eggs, 1 at a time, beating well after each addition.

4 Sift the plain flour, bicarbonate of soda, salt and cinnamon over the butter mixture and stir to blend.

5 ▲ Stir in the wholewheat flour.

6 ▲ With a fork, mash the bananas to a purée, then stir into the mixture. Stir in the vanilla and nuts.

7 ▲ Pour the mixture into the prepared tin and spread level.

8 Bake until a skewer inserted in the centre comes out clean, 50–60 minutes. Let stand 10 minutes before transferring to a rack.

Apricot Nut Loaf

MAKES 1 LOAF

4 oz (115 g) dried apricots
1 large orange
3 oz (85 g) raisins
5 oz (140 g) caster sugar
3 fl oz (85 ml) oil
2 eggs, lightly beaten
9 oz (250 g) plain flour
2 tsp baking powder
½ tsp salt
1 tsp bicarbonate of soda
2 oz (55 g) chopped walnuts

1 Preheat a 350°F/180°C/Gas 4 oven. Line a 9 × 5 in (23 × 13 cm) loaf tin with greaseproof paper and grease.

2 Place the apricots in a bowl, cover with lukewarm water and leave to stand for 30 minutes.

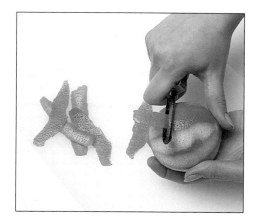

3 ▲ With a vegetable peeler, remove the orange rind, leaving the pith.

4 With a sharp knife, finely chop the orange rind strips.

5 Drain the apricots and chop coarsely. Place in a bowl with the orange rind and raisins. Set aside.

6 Squeeze the peeled orange. Measure the juice and add enough hot water to obtain 6 fl oz (175 ml) liquid.

7 ▼ Pour the orange juice mixture over the apricot mixture. Stir in the sugar, oil and eggs. Set aside.

8 In another bowl, sift together the flour, baking powder, salt and bicarbonate of soda. Fold the flour mixture into the apricot mixture in 3 batches.

9 ▲ Stir in the walnuts.

10 Spoon the mixture into the prepared tin and bake until a skewer inserted in the centre comes out clean, 55–60 minutes. If the loaf browns too quickly, protect the top with a sheet of foil. Let cool in the pan for 10 minutes before transferring to a rack to cool completely.

Bilberry Tea Bread

MAKES 8 PIECES

2 oz (55 g) butter or margarine, at room temperature

6 oz (170 g) caster sugar

1 egg, at room temperature

4 fl oz (125 ml) milk

8 oz (225 g) plain flour

2 tsp baking powder

½ tsp salt

10 oz (285 g) fresh bilberries, or blueberries

FOR THE TOPPING

4 oz (115 g) sugar

1½ oz (45 g) plain flour

½ tsp ground cinnamon

2 oz (55 g) butter, cut in pieces

1 Preheat a 375°F/190°C/Gas 5 oven. Grease a 9 in (23 cm) baking dish.

2 With an electric mixer, cream the butter or margarine with the sugar until light and fluffy. Add the egg, beat to combine, then mix in the milk until blended.

3 ▼ Sift over the flour, baking powder and salt and stir just enough to blend the ingredients.

4 ▲ Add the berries and stir.

5 Transfer to the baking dish.

6 ▲ For the topping, place the sugar, flour, cinnamon and butter in a mixing bowl. Cut in with a pastry blender until the mixture resembles coarse breadcrumbs.

7 ▲ Sprinkle the topping over the mixture in the baking dish.

8 Bake until a skewer inserted in the centre comes out clean, about 45 minutes. Serve warm or cold.

Dried Fruit Loaf

MAKES 1 LOAF

1 lb (450 g) mixed dried fruit, such as currants, raisins, chopped dried apricots and dried cherries
10 fl oz (300 ml) cold strong tea
7 oz (200 g) dark brown sugar
grated rind and juice of 1 small orange
grated rind and juice of 1 lemon
1 egg, lightly beaten
7 oz (200 g) plain flour
1 tbsp baking powder
⅛ tsp salt

1 ▲ In a bowl, mix the dried fruit with the tea and soak overnight.

2 Preheat a 350°F/180°C/Gas 4 oven. Line the bottom and sides of a 9 × 5 in (23 × 13 cm) loaf tin with greaseproof paper and grease the paper.

3 ▲ Strain the fruit, reserving the liquid. In a bowl, combine the sugar, orange and lemon rind, and fruit.

4 ▼ Pour the orange and lemon juice into a measuring jug; if the quantity is less than 8 fl oz (250 ml), top up with the soaking liquid.

5 Stir the citrus juices and egg into the dried fruit mixture.

6 In another bowl, sift together the flour, baking powder and salt. Stir into the fruit mixture until blended.

7 Transfer to the prepared tin and bake until a skewer inserted in the centre comes out clean, about 1¼ hours. Let stand 10 minutes before unmoulding.

Corn Bread

Makes 1 loaf

4 oz (115 g) plain flour
2½ oz (75 g) caster sugar
1 tsp salt
1 tbsp baking powder
6 oz (170 g) cornmeal, or polenta
12 fl oz (350 ml) milk
2 eggs
3 oz (85 g) butter, melted
4 oz (115 g) margarine, melted

1 Preheat a 400°F/200°C/Gas 6 oven. Line a 9 × 5 in (23 × 13 cm) loaf tin with greaseproof paper and grease.

2 Sift the flour, sugar, salt and baking powder into a mixing bowl.

3 ▼ Add the cornmeal and stir to blend. Make a well in the centre.

4 ▲ Whisk together the milk, eggs, butter and margarine. Pour the mixture into the well. Stir until just blended; do not overmix.

5 Pour into the tin and bake until a skewer inserted in the centre comes out clean, about 45 minutes. Serve hot or at room temperature.

Spicy Sweetcorn Bread

Makes 9 squares

3–4 whole canned chilli peppers, drained
2 eggs
16 fl oz (450 ml) buttermilk
2 oz (55 g) butter, melted
2 oz (55 g) plain flour
1 tsp bicarbonate of soda
2 tsp salt
6 oz (170 g) cornmeal, or polenta
12 oz (350 g) canned sweetcorn or frozen sweetcorn, thawed

1 Preheat a 400°F/200°C/Gas 6 oven. Line the bottom and sides of a 9 in (23 cm) square cake tin with greaseproof paper and grease lightly.

2 ▲ With a sharp knife, finely chop the chillis and set aside.

3 ▲ In a large bowl, whisk the eggs until frothy, then whisk in the buttermilk. Add the melted butter.

4 In another large bowl, sift together the flour, bicarbonate of soda and salt. Fold into the buttermilk mixture in 3 batches, then fold in the cornmeal in 3 batches.

5 ▲ Fold in the chillis and sweetcorn.

6 Pour the mixture into the prepared tin and bake until a skewer inserted in the middle comes out clean, 25–30 minutes. Let stand for 2–3 minutes before unmoulding. Cut into squares and serve warm.

Corn Bread (top), Spicy Sweetcorn Bread

Herb Popovers

MAKES 12

3 eggs

8 fl oz (250 ml) milk

1 oz (30 g) butter, melted

3 oz (85 g) plain flour

⅛ tsp salt

1 small sprig each mixed fresh herbs, such as chives, tarragon, dill and parsley

1 Preheat a 425°F/220°C/Gas 7 oven. Grease 12 small ramekins or individual baking cups.

2 With an electric mixer, beat the eggs until blended. Beat in the milk and melted butter.

3 Sift together the flour and salt, then beat into the egg mixture to combine thoroughly.

4 ▼ Strip the herb leaves from the stems and chop finely. Mix together and measure out 2 tablespoons. Stir the herbs into the batter.

5 ▲ Fill the prepared cups half-full.

6 Bake until golden, 25–30 minutes. Do not open the oven door during baking time or the popovers may collapse. For drier popovers, pierce each one with a knife after the 30 minute baking time and bake for 5 minutes more. Serve hot.

Cheese Popovers

MAKES 12

3 eggs

8 fl oz (250 ml) milk

1 oz (30 g) butter, melted

3 oz (85 g) plain flour

¼ tsp salt

¼ tsp paprika

1 oz (30 g) freshly grated Parmesan cheese

~ **VARIATION** ~

For traditional Yorkshire Pudding, omit the cheese and paprika, and use 4–6 tablespoons of beef dripping to replace the butter. Put them into the oven in time to serve warm as an accompaniment for roast beef.

1 Preheat a 425°F/220°C/Gas 7 oven. Grease 12 small ramekins.

2 ▲ With an electric mixer, beat the eggs until blended. Beat in the milk and melted butter.

3 ▲ Sift together the flour, salt and paprika, then beat into the egg mixture. Add the cheese and stir.

4 Fill the prepared cups half-full and bake until golden, 25–30 minutes. Do not open the oven door or the popovers may collapse. For drier popovers, pierce each one with a knife after the 30 minute baking time and bake for 5 minutes more. Serve hot.

Herb Popovers (top), Cheese Popovers

YEAST BREADS

~

*Though the pace of today's life leaves little time for baking,
breadmaking can be very therapeutic. The process is simple
yet infinitely variable, as the loaves that follow prove.
Roll up your sleeves and create a tradition.*

White Bread

MAKES 2 LOAVES

2 fl oz (65 ml) lukewarm water

1 tbsp active dry yeast

2 tbsp caster sugar

16 fl oz (450 ml) lukewarm milk

1 oz (30 g) butter or margarine, at room temperature

2 tsp salt

about 1 lb 14 oz (850 g) strong plain flour

1 Combine the water, yeast and 1 tablespoon of sugar in a measuring jug and let stand 15 minutes until the mixture is frothy.

2 ▼ Pour the milk into a large bowl. Add the remaining sugar, the butter or margarine and salt. Stir in the yeast mixture.

3 Stir in the flour, 5 oz (140 g) at a time, until a stiff dough is obtained. Alternatively, use a food processor.

4 ▲ Transfer the dough to a floured surface. To knead, push the dough away from you with the palm of your hand, then fold it towards you. Repeat until it is smooth and elastic.

5 Place the dough in a large greased bowl, cover with a plastic bag, and leave to rise in a warm place until doubled in volume, 2–3 hours.

6 Grease 2 9 × 5 in (23 × 13 cm) loaf tins.

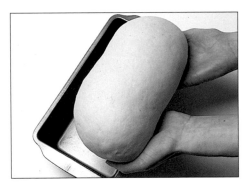

7 ▲ Punch down the risen dough with your fist. Form into loaf shapes and place in the tins, seam-side down. Cover and let rise in a warm place until almost doubled in volume, about 45 minutes.

8 Preheat a 375°F/190°C/Gas 5 oven.

9 Bake until firm and brown, 45–50 minutes. Unmould and tap the bottom of the loaves: if they sound hollow they are done. If necessary, return to the oven and bake a few minutes more. Let cool on a rack.

Country Bread

MAKES 2 LOAVES

12 oz (350 g) wholewheat flour
12 oz (350 g) plain flour
5 oz (140 g) strong plain flour
4 tsp salt
2 oz (55 g) butter, at room temperature
16 fl oz (450 ml) lukewarm milk
FOR THE STARTER
1 tbsp active dry yeast
8 fl oz (250 ml) lukewarm water
5 oz (140 g) plain flour
¼ tsp caster sugar

1 ▲ For the starter, combine the yeast, water, flour and sugar in a bowl and stir with a fork. Cover and leave in a warm place for 2–3 hours, or leave overnight in a cool place.

2 Place the flours, salt and butter in a food processor and process just until blended, 1–2 minutes.

3 Stir together the milk and starter, then slowly pour into the processor, with the motor running, until the mixture forms a dough. If necessary, add more water. Alternatively, the dough can be mixed by hand. Transfer to a floured surface and knead until smooth and elastic.

4 Place in an ungreased bowl, cover with a plastic bag, and leave to rise in a warm place until doubled in volume, about 1½ hours.

5 Transfer to a floured surface and knead briefly. Return to the bowl and leave to rise until tripled in volume, about 1½ hours.

6 ▲ Divide the dough in half. Cut off one-third of the dough from each half and shape into balls. Shape the larger remaining portion of each half into balls. Grease a baking sheet.

7 ▲ For each loaf, top the large ball with the small ball and press the centre with the handle of a wooden spoon to secure. Cover with a plastic bag, slash the top, and leave to rise.

8 Preheat a 400°F/200°C/Gas 6 oven. Dust the dough with flour and bake until the top is browned and the bottom sounds hollow when tapped, 45–50 minutes. Cool on a rack.

Plaited Loaf

MAKES 1 LOAF

1 tbsp active dry yeast

1 tsp honey

8 fl oz (250 ml) lukewarm milk

2 oz (55 g) butter, melted

15 oz (420 g) plain flour

1 tsp salt

1 egg, lightly beaten

1 egg yolk beaten with 1 tsp milk, for glazing

1 ▼ Combine the yeast, honey, milk and butter, stir, and leave for 15 minutes to dissolve.

2 In a large bowl, mix together the flour and salt. Make a well in the centre and add the yeast mixture and egg. With a wooden spoon, stir from the centre, incorporating flour with each turn, to obtain a rough dough.

3 Transfer to a floured surface and knead until smooth and elastic. Place in a clean bowl, cover, and leave to rise in a warm place until doubled in volume, about 1½ hours.

4 Grease a baking sheet. Punch down the dough and divide into three equal pieces. Roll to shape each piece into a long thin strip.

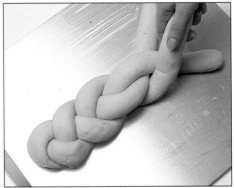

5 ▲ Begin plaiting from the centre strip, tucking in the ends. Cover loosely and leave to rise in a warm place for 30 minutes.

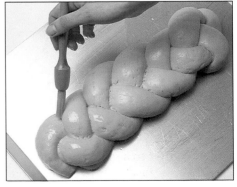

6 ▲ Preheat a 375°F/190°C/Gas 5 oven. Place the bread in a cool place while the oven heats. Brush with the glaze and bake until golden, 40–45 minutes. Set on a rack to cool.

Sesame Seed Bread

MAKES 1 LOAF

2 tsp active dry yeast
10 fl oz (300 ml) lukewarm water
7 oz (200 g) plain flour
7 oz (200 g) wholewheat flour
2 tsp salt
2½ oz (70 g) toasted sesame seeds
milk, for glazing
2 tbsp sesame seeds, for sprinkling

1 Combine the yeast and 5 tbsp of the water and leave to dissolve. Mix the flours and salt in a large bowl. Make a well in the centre and pour in the yeast and water.

2 ▲ With a wooden spoon, stir from the centre, incorporating flour with each turn, to obtain a rough dough.

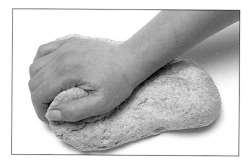

3 ▲ Transfer to a floured surface. To knead, push the dough away from you with the palm of your hand, then fold it towards you and push away again. Repeat until smooth and elastic, then return to the bowl and cover with a plastic bag. Leave in a warm place until doubled in volume, 1½–2 hours.

4 ▲ Grease a 9 in (23 cm) cake tin. Punch down the dough and knead in the sesame seeds. Divide the dough into 16 balls and place in the pan. Cover with a plastic bag and leave in a warm place until risen above the rim of the tin.

5 ▼ Preheat a 425°F/220°C/Gas 7 oven. Brush the loaf with milk and sprinkle with the sesame seeds. Bake for 15 minutes. Lower the heat to 375°F/190°C/Gas 5 and bake until the bottom sounds hollow when tapped, about 30 minutes more. Cool on a rack.

Wholewheat Bread

MAKES 1 LOAF

1 lb 5 oz (600 g) wholewheat flour
2 tsp salt
4 tsp active dry yeast
15 fl oz (425 ml) lukewarm water
2 tbsp honey
3 tbsp oil
1½ oz (45 g) wheatgerm
milk, for glazing

1 Combine the flour and salt in a bowl and place in the oven at its lowest setting until warmed, 8–10 minutes.

2 Meanwhile, combine the yeast with half of the water in a small bowl and leave to dissolve.

3 ▼ Make a well in the centre of the flour. Pour in the yeast mixture, the remaining water, honey, oil and wheatgerm. With a wooden spoon, stir from the centre until smooth.

4 Transfer the dough to a lightly floured surface and knead just enough to shape into a loaf.

5 ▲ Grease a 9 × 5 in (23 × 13 cm) loaf tin, place the dough in it and cover with a plastic bag. Leave in a warm place until the dough is about 1 in (2.5 cm) higher than the tin rim, about 1 hour.

6 Preheat a 400°F/200°C/Gas 6 oven. Bake until the bottom sounds hollow when tapped, 35–40 minutes. Cool.

Rye Bread

MAKES 1 LOAF

7 oz (200 g) rye flour
16 fl oz (450 ml) boiling water
4 fl oz (125 ml) black treacle
2½ oz (70 g) butter, cut in pieces
1 tbsp salt
2 tbsp caraway seeds
1 tbsp active dry yeast
4 fl oz (125 ml) lukewarm water
about 1 lb 14 oz (850 g) plain flour
semolina or flour, for dusting

~ COOK'S TIP ~

To bring out the flavour of the caraway seeds, toast them lightly. Spread the seeds on a baking tray and place in a preheated 325°F/170°C/Gas 3 oven for about 7 minutes.

1 ▲ Mix the rye flour, boiling water, treacle, butter, salt and caraway seeds in a large bowl. Leave to cool.

2 In another bowl, mix the yeast and lukewarm water and leave to dissolve. Stir into the rye flour mixture. Stir in just enough plain flour to obtain a stiff dough. If it becomes too stiff, stir with your hands.

3 Transfer to a floured surface and knead until the dough is no longer sticky and is smooth and shiny.

4 Place in a greased bowl, cover with a plastic bag, and leave in a warm place until doubled in volume. Punch down the dough, cover, and let rise again for 30 minutes.

5 Preheat a 350°F/180°C/Gas 4 oven. Dust a baking sheet with semolina.

6 ▼ Shape the dough into a ball. Place on the sheet and score several times across the top. Bake until the bottom sounds hollow when tapped, about 40 minutes. Cool on a rack.

Wholewheat Bread (top), Rye Bread

Potato Bread

MAKES 2 LOAVES

4 tsp active dry yeast
8 fl oz (250 ml) lukewarm milk
8 oz (225 g) potatoes, boiled (reserve 8 fl oz (250 ml) of potato cooking liquid)
2 tbsp oil
4 tsp salt
1 lb 14 oz–2 lb (850–900 g) plain flour

1 Combine the yeast and milk in a large bowl and leave to dissolve, about 15 minutes.

2 Meanwhile, mash the potatoes.

3 ▲ Add the potatoes, oil and salt to the yeast mixture and mix well. Stir in the reserved cooking water, then stir in the flour, in 6 separate batches, to form a stiff dough.

4 Transfer to a floured surface and knead until smooth and elastic. Return to the bowl, cover, and leave in a warm place until doubled in size, 1–1½ hours. Punch down, then leave to rise for another 40 minutes.

5 Grease 2 9 × 5 in (23 × 13 cm) loaf tins. Roll the dough into 20 small balls. Place 2 rows of balls in each tin. Leave until the dough has risen above the rim of the tins.

6 Preheat a 400°F/200°C/Gas 6 oven. Bake for 10 minutes, then lower the heat to 375°F/190°C/Gas 5. Bake until the bottoms sound hollow when tapped, 40 minutes. Cool on a rack.

Irish Soda Bread

MAKES 1 LOAF

10 oz (285 g) plain flour
5 oz (140 g) wholewheat flour
1 tsp bicarbonate of soda
1 tsp salt
1 oz (30 g) butter or margarine, at room temperature
10 fl oz (300 ml) buttermilk
1 tbsp plain flour, for dusting

1 Preheat a 400°F/200°C/Gas 6 oven. Grease a baking sheet.

2 Sift the flours, bicarbonate of soda and salt together into a bowl. Make a well in the centre and add the butter or margarine and buttermilk. Working outwards from the centre, stir with a fork until a soft dough is formed.

3 ▲ With floured hands, gather the dough into a ball.

4 ▲ Transfer to a floured surface and knead for 3 minutes. Shape the dough into a large round.

5 ▲ Place on the baking sheet. Cut a cross in the top with a sharp knife.

6 ▲ Dust with flour. Bake until brown, 40–50 minutes. Transfer to a rack to cool.

Potato Bread (top), Irish Soda Bread

Wholewheat Rolls

MAKES 12

2 tsp active dry yeast
2 fl oz (65 ml) lukewarm water
1 tsp caster sugar
6 fl oz (175 ml) lukewarm buttermilk
¼ tsp bicarbonate of soda
1 tsp salt
1½ oz (45 g) butter, at room temperature
7 oz (200 g) wholewheat flour
5 oz (140 g) plain flour
1 beaten egg, for glazing

1 In a large bowl, combine the yeast, water and sugar. Stir, and leave for 15 minutes to dissolve.

2 ▲ Add the buttermilk, bicarbonate of soda, salt and butter and stir to blend. Stir in the wholewheat flour.

3 Add just enough of the plain flour to obtain a rough dough.

4 Transfer to a floured surface and knead until smooth and elastic. Divide into 3 equal parts. Roll each into a cylinder, then cut in 4.

5 ▼ Form the pieces into torpedo shapes. Place on a greased baking sheet, cover and leave in a warm place until doubled in volume.

6 Preheat a 400°F/200°C/Gas 6 oven. Brush the rolls with the glaze. Bake until firm, 15–20 minutes. Cool on a rack.

French Bread

MAKES 2 LOAVES

1 tbsp active dry yeast
16 fl oz (450 ml) lukewarm water
1 tbsp salt
1 lb 14 oz–2 lb 8 oz (850 g–1.2 kg) plain flour
semolina or flour, for sprinkling

1 Combine the yeast and water, stir, and leave for 15 minutes to dissolve. Stir in the salt.

2 Add the flour, 5 oz (140 g) at a time. Beat in with a wooden spoon, adding just enough flour to obtain a smooth dough. Alternatively, use an electric mixer with a dough hook.

3 Transfer to a floured surface and knead until smooth and elastic.

4 Shape into a ball, place in a greased bowl and cover with a plastic bag. Leave to rise in a warm place until doubled in volume, 2–4 hours.

5 ▲ Transfer to a lightly floured board and shape into 2 long loaves. Place on a baking sheet sprinkled with semolina or flour and let rise for 5 minutes.

6 ▲ Score the tops in several places with a very sharp knife. Brush with water and place in a cold oven. Set a pan of boiling water on the bottom of the oven and set the oven to 400°F/200°C/Gas 6. Bake until crusty and golden, about 40 minutes. Cool on a rack.

Wholewheat Rolls (top), French Bread

Poppyseed Knots

MAKES 12

10 fl oz (300 ml) lukewarm milk

2 oz (55 g) butter, at room temperature

1 tsp caster sugar

2 tsp active dry yeast

1 egg yolk

2 tsp salt

1 lb 2 oz–1 lb 4 oz (500–575 g) plain flour

1 egg beaten with 2 tsp of water, for glazing

poppyseeds, for sprinkling

1 In a large bowl, stir together the milk, butter, sugar and yeast. Leave for 15 minutes to dissolve.

2 Stir in the egg yolk, salt and 10 oz (285 g) flour. Add half the remaining flour and stir to obtain a soft dough.

3 Transfer to a floured surface and knead, adding flour if necessary, until smooth and elastic. Place in a bowl, cover and leave in a warm place until doubled in volume, 1½–2 hours.

4 ▲ Grease a baking sheet. Punch down the dough with your fist and cut into 12 pieces the size of golf balls.

5 ▲ Roll each piece to a rope, twist to form a knot and place 1 in (2.5 cm) apart on the sheet. Cover loosely and leave to rise in a warm place until doubled in volume, 1–1½ hours.

6 Preheat a 350°F/180°C/Gas 4 oven.

7 ▲ Brush the knots with the egg glaze and sprinkle over the poppyseeds. Bake until the tops are lightly browned, 25–30 minutes. Cool slightly on a rack before serving.

Clover Leaf Rolls

MAKES 24

10 fl oz (300 ml) milk

2 tbsp caster sugar

2 oz (55 g) butter, at room temperature,

2 tsp active dry yeast

1 egg

2 tsp salt

1 lb 2 oz–1 lb 4 oz (500–575 g) plain flour

melted butter, for glazing

1 ▲ Heat the milk until lukewarm; test the temperature with your knuckle. Pour into a large bowl and stir in the sugar, butter and yeast. Leave for 15 minutes to dissolve.

2 Stir the egg and salt into the yeast mixture. Gradually stir in 1 lb 2 oz (500 g) of the flour. Add just enough extra flour to obtain a rough dough.

3 ▲ Transfer to a floured surface and knead until smooth and elastic. Place in a greased bowl, cover and leave in a warm place until doubled in volume, about 1½ hours.

4 Grease 2 12-cup bun trays.

5 ▼ Punch down the dough. Cut into 4 equal pieces. Roll each piece into a rope 14 in (35 cm) long. Cut each rope into 18 pieces, then roll each into a ball.

6 ▲ Place 3 balls, side by side, in each bun cup. Cover loosely and leave to rise in a warm place until doubled in volume, about 1½ hours.

7 Preheat a 400°F/200°C/Gas 6 oven.

8 Brush the rolls with glaze. Bake until lightly browned, about 20 minutes. Cool slightly before serving.

Croissants

MAKES 18

1 tbsp active dry yeast
11 fl oz (335 ml) lukewarm milk
2 tsp caster sugar
1½ tsp salt
15 oz–1 lb 2 oz (420–500 g) plain flour
8 oz (225 g) cold unsalted butter
1 egg beaten with 2 tsp water, for glazing

1 In the large bowl of an electric mixer, stir together the yeast and warm milk. Leave for 15 minutes to dissolve. Stir in the sugar, salt and 5 oz (140 g) of the flour.

2 Using a dough hook, on low speed, gradually add the remaining flour. Beat on high until the dough pulls away from the sides of the bowl. Cover and let rise in a warm place until doubled, about 1½ hours.

3 On a floured surface, knead the dough until smooth. Wrap in greaseproof paper and refrigerate for 15 minutes.

4 ▲ Divide the butter into 2 halves and place each between 2 sheets of greaseproof paper. With a rolling pin, flatten each to form a 6 × 4 in (15 × 10 cm) rectangle. Set aside.

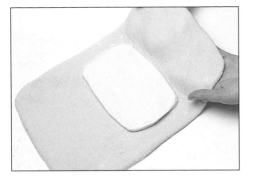

5 ▲ On a floured surface, roll out the dough to 12 × 8 in (30 × 20 cm). Place a butter rectangle in the centre. Fold the bottom third of dough over the butter and press gently to seal. Top with the other butter rectangle, then fold over the top dough third.

6 ▲ Turn the dough so that the short side is facing you, with the long folded edge on the left and the long open edge on the right, like a book.

7 Roll the dough gently into a 12 × 8 in (30 × 20 cm) rectangle; do not press the butter out. Fold in thirds again and mark one corner with your fingertip to indicate the first turn. Wrap and refrigerate for 30 minutes.

8 Repeat twice more: again position the dough like a book, roll, fold in thirds, mark, wrap, and chill. After the third fold, refrigerate at least 2 hours (or overnight).

9 Roll out the dough about ⅛ in (3 mm) thick to a rectangle about 13 in (33 cm) wide. Trim the sides to neaten.

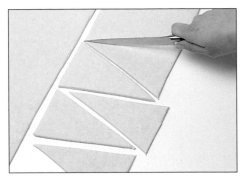

10 ▲ Cut the dough in half lengthwise, then cut into triangles 6 in (15 cm) high with a 4 in (10 cm) base.

11 ▲ Gently go over the triangles lengthwise with a rolling pin to stretch slightly. Roll up from base to point. Place point-down on baking sheets and curve to form a crescent. Cover and let rise in a warm place until more than doubled in volume, 1–1½ hours. (Or, refrigerate overnight and bake the next day.)

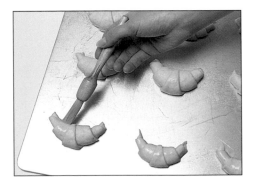

12 ▲ Preheat a 475°F/240°C/Gas 9 oven. Brush with the glaze. Bake for 2 minutes. Lower the heat to 375°F/190°C/Gas 5 and bake until golden, 10–12 more minutes. Serve warm.

Pizza

MAKES 2

1 lb 2 oz (500 g) plain flour
1 tsp salt
2 tsp active dry yeast
10 fl oz (300 ml) lukewarm water
2–4 fl oz (65–125 ml) extra-virgin olive oil
tomato sauce, grated cheese, olives and herbs, for topping

1 Combine the flour and salt in a large mixing bowl. Make a well in the centre and add the yeast, water and 2 tablespoons of the olive oil. Leave for 15 minutes to dissolve the yeast.

2 With your hands, stir until the dough just holds together. Transfer to a floured surface and knead until smooth and elastic. Avoid adding too much flour while kneading.

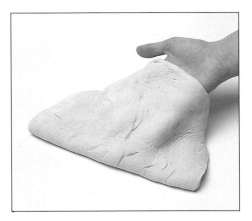

3 ▲ Brush the inside of a clean bowl with 1 tablespoon of the oil. Place the dough in the bowl and roll around to coat with the oil. Cover with a plastic bag and leave to rise in a warm place until more than doubled in volume, about 45 minutes.

4 Divide the dough into 2 balls. Preheat a 400°F/200°C/Gas 6 oven.

5 ▲ Roll each ball into a 10 in (25 cm) circle. Flip the circles over and onto your palm. Set each circle on the work surface and rotate, stretching the dough as you turn, until it is about 12 in (30 cm) in diameter.

6 ▲ Brush 2 pizza pans with oil. Place the dough circles in the pans and neaten the edges. Brush with oil.

7 ▲ Cover with the toppings and bake until golden, 10–12 minutes.

Bread Sticks

MAKES 18–20

1 tbsp active dry yeast
10 fl oz (300 ml) lukewarm water
15 oz (420 g) plain flour
2 tsp salt
1 tsp caster sugar
2 tbsp olive oil
5 oz (140 g) sesame seeds
1 beaten egg, for glazing
coarse salt, for sprinkling

1 Combine the yeast and water, stir and leave for 15 minutes to dissolve.

2 ▲ Place the flour, salt, sugar and olive oil in a food processor. With the motor running, slowly pour in the yeast mixture and process until the dough forms a ball. If sticky, add more flour; if dry, add more water.

3 Transfer to a floured surface and knead until smooth and elastic. Place in a bowl, cover and leave to rise in a warm place for 45 minutes.

4 ▲ Lightly toast the sesame seeds in a frying pan. Grease 2 baking sheets.

5 ▼ Roll small handfuls of dough into cylinders, about 12 in (30 cm) long. Place on the baking sheets.

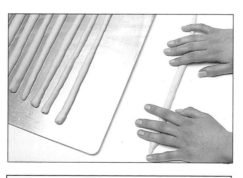

~ **VARIATION** ~

If preferred, use other seeds, such as poppy or caraway, or for plain bread sticks, omit the seeds and salt.

6 ▲ Brush with egg glaze, sprinkle with the sesame seeds, then sprinkle over some coarse salt. Leave to rise, uncovered, until almost doubled in volume, about 20 minutes.

7 Preheat a 400°F/200°C/Gas 6 oven. Bake until golden, about 15 minutes. Turn off the heat but leave the bread sticks in the oven for 5 minutes more. Serve warm or cool.

Plaited Prune Bread

MAKES 1 LOAF

1 tbsp active dry yeast
2 fl oz (65 ml) lukewarm water
2 fl oz (65 ml) lukewarm milk
2 oz (55 g) caster sugar
½ tsp salt
1 egg
2 oz (55 g) butter, at room temperature
15 oz–1 lb 2 oz (420–500 g) plain flour
1 egg beaten with 2 tsp water, for glazing
FOR THE FILLING
7 oz (200 g) cooked prunes
2 tsp grated lemon rind
1 tsp grated orange rind
¼ tsp freshly grated nutmeg
1½ oz (45 g) butter, melted
2 oz (55 g) very finely chopped walnuts
2 tbsp caster sugar

1 In a large bowl, combine the yeast and water, stir and leave for 15 minutes to dissolve.

2 Stir in the milk, sugar, salt, egg and butter. Gradually stir in 12 oz (350 g) of the flour to obtain a soft dough.

3 Transfer to a floured surface and knead in just enough flour to obtain a dough that is smooth and elastic. Put into a clean bowl, cover and leave to rise in a warm place until doubled in volume, about 1½ hours.

~ VARIATION ~

For Plaited Apricot Bread, replace the prunes with the same amount of dried apricots. It is not necessary to cook them, but to soften, soak them in hot tea and discard the liquid before using.

4 ▲ Meanwhile, for the filling, combine the prunes, lemon and orange rinds, nutmeg, butter, walnuts and sugar and stir together to blend. Set aside.

5 Grease a large baking sheet. Punch down the dough and transfer to a lightly floured surface. Knead briefly, then roll out into a 15 × 10 in (38 × 25 cm) rectangle. Carefully transfer to the baking sheet.

6 ▲ Spread the filling in the centre.

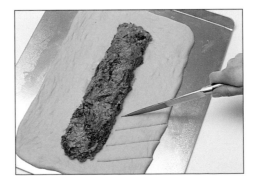

7 ▲ With a sharp knife, cut 10 strips at an angle on either side of the filling, cutting just to the filling.

8 ▲ For a plaited pattern, fold up one end neatly, then fold over the strips from alternating sides until all the strips are folded over. Tuck excess dough underneath at the ends.

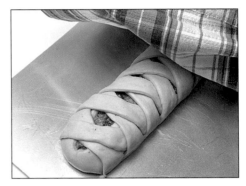

9 ▲ Cover loosely with a tea towel and leave to rise in a warm place until almost doubled in volume.

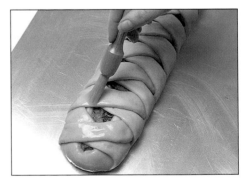

10 ▲ Preheat a 375°F/190°C/Gas 5 oven. Brush with the glaze. Bake until browned, about 30 minutes. Transfer to a rack to cool.

PIES & TARTS

~

*Here is every sort of filling – from orchard fruits to
autumn nuts, tangy citrus to luscious chocolate – for the
most memorable pies and tarts. Some are plain and
some are fancy, but all are delicious.*

Apple Pie

SERVES 8

2 lb (900 g) tart cooking apples
2 tbsp plain flour
4 oz (115 g) caster sugar
1½ tbsp fresh lemon juice
½ tsp ground cinnamon
½ tsp ground allspice
¼ tsp ground ginger
¼ tsp grated nutmeg
¼ tsp salt
2 oz (55 g) butter, diced
FOR THE PASTRY
10 oz (285 g) plain flour
1 tsp salt
3 oz (85 g) cold butter, cut in pieces
2 oz (55 g) cold vegetable fat or lard, cut in pieces
2–4 fl oz (65–125 ml) iced water

1 ▲ For the crust, sift the flour and salt into a bowl.

2 Add the butter and fat and cut in with a pastry blender or rub between your fingertips until the mixture resembles coarse breadcrumbs. With a fork, stir in just enough water to bind the pastry.

3 ▲ Form 2 balls, wrap in greaseproof paper and refrigerate for 20 minutes.

4 ▲ On a lightly floured surface, roll out 1 ball ⅛ in (3 mm) thick. Transfer to a 9 in (23 cm) pie dish and trim the edge. Preheat a baking sheet in the centre of a 425°F/220°C/Gas 7 oven.

5 ▲ Peel, core and slice the apples into a bowl. Toss with the flour, sugar, lemon juice, spices and salt. Spoon into pie shell; dot with butter.

6 ▲ Roll out the remaining pastry. Place on top of the pie and trim to leave a ¾ in (2 cm) overhang. Fold the overhang under the pastry base and press to seal. Crimp the edge.

7 ▲ Roll out the scraps and cut out leaf shapes and roll balls. Arrange on top of the pie. Cut steam vents.

8 Bake for 10 minutes. Reduce the heat to 350°F/180°C/Gas 4 and bake until golden, 40–45 minutes more. If the pie browns too quickly, protect with foil.

~ **COOK'S TIP** ~

Instead of using cooking apples, choose crisp eaters such as Granny Smith, that will not soften too much during cooking.

Plum Pie

SERVES 8

2 lb (900 g) red or purple plums

grated rind of 1 lemon

1 tbsp fresh lemon juice

4–6 oz (115–170 g) caster sugar

3 tbsp quick-cooking tapioca

⅛ tsp salt

½ tsp ground cinnamon

¼ tsp grated nutmeg

FOR THE PASTRY

10 oz (285 g) plain flour

1 tsp salt

3 oz (85 g) cold butter, cut in pieces

2 oz (55 g) cold vegetable fat or lard, cut in pieces

2–4 fl oz (65–125 ml) iced water

milk, for glazing

1 ▼ For the pastry, sift the flour and salt into a bowl. Add the butter and fat and cut in with a pastry blender until the mixture resembles coarse breadcrumbs.

2 Stir in just enough water to bind the pastry. Gather into 2 balls, 1 slightly larger than the other. Wrap and refrigerate for 20 minutes.

3 Preheat a baking sheet in the centre of a 425°F/220°C/Gas 7 oven.

4 On a lightly floured surface, roll out the larger pastry ball to about ⅛ in (3 mm) thick. Transfer to a 9 in (23 cm) pie dish and trim the edge.

5 ▲ Halve the plums, discard the stones, and cut in large pieces. Mix all the filling ingredients together (if the plums are very tart, use extra sugar). Transfer to the pastry case.

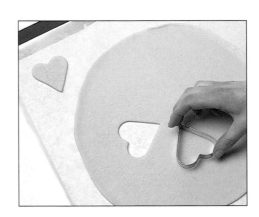

6 ▲ Roll out the remaining pastry and place on a baking tray lined with greaseproof paper. With a cutter, stamp out 4 hearts. Transfer the pastry lid to the pie using the paper.

7 Trim to leave a ¾ in (2 cm) overhang. Fold the top edge under the bottom and pinch to seal. Arrange the hearts on top. Brush with the milk. Bake for 15 minutes. Reduce the heat to 350°F/180°C/Gas 4 and bake 30–35 minutes more. If the crust browns too quickly, protect with a sheet of foil.

Lattice Berry Pie

SERVES 8

1 lb (450 g) berries, such as bilberries, blueberries, blackcurrants etc
4 oz (115 g) caster sugar
3 tbsp cornflour
2 tbsp fresh lemon juice
1 oz (30 g) butter, diced
FOR THE PASTRY
10 oz (285 g) plain flour
¾ tsp salt
4 oz (115 g) cold butter, cut in pieces
1½ oz (45 g) cold vegetable fat or lard, cut in pieces
5–6 tbsp iced water
1 egg beaten with 1 tbsp water, for glazing

1 For the pastry, sift the flour and salt into a bowl. Add the butter and fat and cut in with a pastry blender until the mixture resembles coarse breadcrumbs. With a fork, stir in just enough water to bind the pastry. Form into 2 balls, wrap in greaseproof paper, and refrigerate for 20 minutes.

2 On a lightly floured surface, roll out one ball about ⅛ in (3 mm) thick. Transfer to a 9 in (23 cm) pie dish and trim to leave a ½ in (1 cm) overhang. Brush the bottom with egg glaze.

3 ▲ Mix all the filling ingredients together, except the butter (reserve a few berries for decoration). Spoon into the pastry case and dot with the butter. Brush the egg glaze around the rim of the pastry case.

4 Preheat a baking sheet in the centre of a 425°F/220°C/Gas 7 oven.

5 ▼ Roll out the remaining pastry on a baking tray lined with greaseproof paper. With a serrated pastry wheel, cut out 24 thin pastry strips. Roll out the scraps and cut out leaf shapes. Mark veins in the leaves with the point of a knife.

6 ▲ Weave the strips in a close lattice, then transfer to the pie using the paper. Press the edges to seal and trim. Arrange the pastry leaves around the rim. Brush with egg glaze.

7 Bake for 10 minutes. Reduce the heat to 350°F/180°C/Gas 4 and bake until the pastry is golden, 40–45 minutes more. Decorate with berries.

Raspberry Tart

SERVES 8

4 egg yolks

2½ oz (70 g) caster sugar

3 tbsp plain flour

10 fl oz (300 ml) milk

⅛ tsp salt

½ tsp vanilla essence

1 lb (450 g) fresh raspberries

5 tbsp red currant jelly

1 tbsp fresh orange juice

FOR THE PASTRY

6½ oz (190 g) plain flour

½ tsp baking powder

¼ tsp salt

1 tbsp sugar

grated rind of ½ orange

3 oz (85 g) cold butter, cut in pieces

1 egg yolk

3–4 tbsp whipping cream

1 For the pastry, sift the flour, baking powder and salt into a bowl. Stir in the sugar and orange rind. Add the butter and cut in with a pastry blender until the mixture resembles coarse breadcrumbs. Stir in the egg yolk and just enough cream to bind the dough. Gather into a ball, wrap in greaseproof paper and refrigerate.

2 For the custard filling, beat the egg yolks and sugar until thick and lemon-coloured. Gradually stir in the flour.

3 In a saucepan, bring the milk and salt just to the boil, then remove from the heat. Whisk into the egg yolk mixture, return to the pan and continue whisking over moderately high heat until just bubbling. Cook for 3 minutes to thicken. Transfer immediately to a bowl. Add the vanilla and stir to blend.

4 ▲ Cover with greaseproof paper to prevent a skin from forming.

5 ▲ Preheat a 400°F/200°C/Gas 6 oven. On a floured surface, roll out the pastry ⅛ in (3 mm) thick, transfer to a 10 in (25 cm) pie dish and trim. Prick the bottom with a fork and line with crumpled greaseproof. Fill with baking beans and bake for 15 minutes. Remove the paper and beans. Continue baking until golden, 6–8 minutes more. Let cool.

6 ▲ Spread an even layer of the pastry cream filling in the pastry case and arrange the raspberries on top. Melt the jelly and orange juice in a pan and brush on top to glaze.

Rhubarb and Cherry Pie

1 lb (450 g) rhubarb, cut into 1 in (2.5 cm) pieces
1 lb (450 g) canned stoned tart red or black cherries, drained
10 oz (285 g) caster sugar
1 oz (30 g) quick-cooking tapioca
FOR THE PASTRY
10 oz (285 g) plain flour
1 tsp salt
3 oz (85 g) cold butter, cut in pieces
2 oz (55 g) cold vegetable fat or lard, cut in pieces
2–4 fl oz (65–125 ml) iced water
milk, for glazing

1 ▲ For the pastry, sift the flour and salt into a bowl. Add the butter and fat to the dry ingredients and cut in with a pastry blender until the mixture resembles coarse breadcrumbs.

2 With a fork, stir in just enough water to bind the pastry. Gather into 2 balls, 1 slightly larger than the other. Wrap the pastry in greaseproof paper and refrigerate for at least 20 minutes.

3 Preheat a baking sheet in the centre of a 400°F/200°C/Gas 6 oven.

4 On a lightly floured surface, roll out the larger pastry ball to a thickness of about ⅛ in (3 mm).

5 ▼ Roll the pastry around the rolling pin and transfer to a 9 in (23 cm) pie dish. Trim the edge to leave a ½ in (1 cm) overhang.

6 Refrigerate the pastry case while making the filling.

7 In a mixing bowl, combine the rhubarb, cherries, sugar and tapioca and spoon into the pie shell.

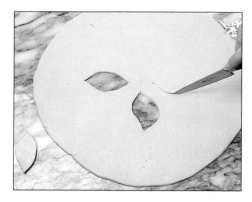

8 ▲ Roll out the remaining pastry and cut out leaf shapes.

9 Transfer the pastry lid to the pie and trim to leave a ¾ in (2 cm) overhang. Fold the top edge under the bottom and flute. Roll small balls from the scraps. Mark veins in the pastry leaves and place on top with the balls.

10 Glaze the top and bake until golden, 40–50 minutes.

Peach Tart with Almond Cream

SERVES 8–10

4 large ripe peaches
4 oz (115 g) blanched almonds
2 tbsp plain flour
3½ oz (100 g) unsalted butter, at room temperature
4 oz (115 g) plus 2 tbsp caster sugar
1 egg
1 egg yolk
½ tsp vanilla essence, or 2 tsp rum
FOR THE PASTRY
6½ oz (190 g) plain flour
¾ tsp salt
3½ oz (100 g) cold unsalted butter, cut in pieces
1 egg yolk
2½–3 tbsp iced water

4 ▲ On a floured surface, roll out the pastry ⅛ in (3 mm) thick. Transfer to a 10 in (25 cm) pie dish. Trim the edge, prick the bottom and refrigerate.

5 ▲ Score the bottoms of the peaches. Drop the peaches, 1 at a time, into boiling water. Boil for 20 seconds, then dip in cold water. Peel off the skins using a sharp knife.

7 ▲ Halve the peaches and remove the stones. Cut crosswise in thin slices and arrange on top of the almond cream like the spokes of a wheel; keep the slices of each peach-half together. Fan out by pressing down gently at a slight angle.

8 ▲ Bake until the pastry begins to brown, 10–15 minutes. Lower the heat to 350°F/180°C/Gas 4 and continue baking until the almond cream sets, about 15 minutes more. Ten minutes before the end of the cooking time, sprinkle with the remaining 2 tablespoons of sugar.

~ **VARIATION** ~

For a Nectarine and Apricot Tart with Almond Cream, replace the peaches with nectarines, prepared and arranged the same way. Peel and chop 3 fresh apricots. Fill the spaces between the fanned-out nectarines with 1 tablespoon of chopped apricots. Bake as above.

1 ▲ For the pastry, sift the flour and salt into a bowl.

2 Add the butter and cut in with a pastry blender until the mixture resembles coarse breadcrumbs. Stir in the egg yolk and just enough water to bind the pastry. Gather into a ball, wrap in greaseproof paper, and refrigerate for at least 20 minutes.

3 Preheat a baking sheet in the centre of a 400°F/200°C/Gas 6 oven.

6 ▲ Grind the almonds finely with the flour in a food processor, blender or grinder. With an electric mixer, cream the butter and 4 oz (115 g) of the sugar until light and fluffy. Gradually beat in the egg and yolk. Stir in the almonds and vanilla or rum. Spread in the pastry case.

Pear and Apple Crumble Pie

SERVES 8

3 firm pears

4 cooking apples

6 oz (170 g) caster sugar

2 tbsp cornflour

1/8 tsp salt

grated rind of 1 lemon

2 tbsp fresh lemon juice

3 oz (85 g) raisins

3 oz (85 g) plain flour

1 tsp ground cinnamon

3 oz (85 g) cold butter, cut in pieces

FOR THE PASTRY

5 oz (140 g) plain flour

1/2 tsp salt

2 1/2 oz (70 g) cold vegetable fat or lard,
   cut in pieces

2 tbsp iced water

1 For the pastry, combine the flour and salt in a bowl. Add the fat and cut in with a pastry blender until the mixture resembles coarse breadcrumbs. Stir in just enough water to bind the pastry. Gather into a ball and transfer to a lightly floured surface. Roll out 1/8 in (3 mm) thick.

2 ▲ Transfer to a shallow 9 in (23 cm) pie dish and trim to leave a 1/2 in (1 cm) overhang. Fold the overhang under for double thickness. Flute the edge. Refrigerate.

3 Preheat a baking sheet in the centre of a 450°F/230°C/Gas 8 oven.

4 ▲ Peel and core the pears. Slice them into a bowl. Peel, core and slice the apples. Add to the pears. Stir in one-third of the sugar, the cornflour, salt and lemon rind. Add the lemon juice and raisins and stir to blend.

5 For the crumble topping, combine the remaining sugar, flour, cinnamon, and butter in a bowl. Blend with your fingertips until the mixture resembles coarse breadcrumbs. Set aside.

6 ▲ Spoon the fruit filling into the pastry case. Sprinkle the crumbs lightly and evenly over the top.

7 Bake for 10 minutes, then reduce the heat to 350°F/180°C/Gas 4. Cover the top of the pie loosely with a sheet of foil and continue baking until browned, 35–40 minutes more.

Chocolate Pear Tart

SERVES 8

| 4 oz (115 g) plain chocolate, grated |
| 3 large firm, ripe pears |
| 1 egg |
| 1 egg yolk |
| 4 fl oz (125 ml) single cream |
| ½ tsp vanilla essence |
| 3 tbsp caster sugar |
| FOR THE PASTRY |
| 5 oz (140 g) plain flour |
| ⅛ tsp salt |
| 2 tbsp sugar |
| 4 oz (115 g) cold unsalted butter, cut into pieces |
| 1 egg yolk |
| 1 tbsp fresh lemon juice |

1 For the pastry, sift the flour and salt into a bowl. Add the sugar and butter. Cut in with a pastry blender until the mixture resembles coarse breadcrumbs. Stir in the egg yolk and lemon juice until the mixture forms a ball. Wrap in greaseproof paper, and refrigerate for at least 20 minutes.

2 Preheat a baking sheet in the centre of a 400°F/200°C/Gas 6 oven.

3 On a lightly floured surface, roll out the pastry ⅛ in (3 mm) thick. Transfer to a 10 in (25 cm) tart dish and trim.

4 ▲ Sprinkle the bottom of the case with the grated chocolate.

5 ▲ Peel, halve and core the pears. Cut in thin slices crosswise, then fan them out slightly.

6 Transfer the pear halves to the tart with the help of a metal spatula and arrange on top of the chocolate like the spokes of a wheel.

7 ▼ Whisk together the egg and egg yolk, cream and vanilla. Ladle over the pears, then sprinkle with sugar.

8 Bake for 10 minutes. Reduce the heat to 350°F/180°C/Gas 4 and cook until the custard is set and the pears begin to caramelize, about 20 minutes more. Serve warm.

Lime Tart

SERVES 8

3 large egg yolks

1 × 14 oz (400 g) can sweetened
  condensed milk

1 tbsp grated lime rind

4 fl oz (125 ml) fresh lime juice

green food colouring (optional)

4 fl oz (125 ml) whipping cream

FOR THE BASE

4 oz (115 g) digestive biscuits, crushed

2½ oz (70 g) butter or margarine, melted

1 Preheat a 350°F/180°C/Gas 4 oven.

2 ▲ For the base, place the crushed
biscuits in a bowl and add the butter
or margarine. Mix to combine.

~ **VARIATION** ~

Use lemons instead of limes,
with yellow food colouring.

3 Press the mixture evenly over the
bottom and sides of a 9 in (23 cm) pie
dish. Bake for 8 minutes. Let cool.

4 ▲ Beat the yolks until thick. Beat
in the milk, lime rind and juice and
colouring, if using. Pour into the
pastry case and refrigerate until set,
about 4 hours. To serve, whip the
cream. Pipe a lattice pattern on top,
or spoon dollops around the edge.

Fruit Tartlets

MAKES 8

6 fl oz (175 ml) red currant jelly

1 tbsp fresh lemon juice

6 fl oz (175 ml) whipping cream

1½ lb (700 g) fresh fruit, such as
  strawberries, raspberries, kiwi fruit,
  peaches, grapes or currants, peeled
  and sliced as necessary

FOR THE PASTRY

5 oz (140 g) cold butter, cut in pieces

2½ oz (65 g) dark brown sugar

3 tbsp cocoa powder

7 oz (200 g) plain flour

1 egg white

1 For the pastry, combine the butter,
brown sugar and cocoa over low heat.
When the butter is melted, remove
from the heat and sift over the flour.
Stir, then add just enough egg white
to bind the mixture. Gather into a
ball, wrap in greaseproof paper, and
refrigerate for 30 minutes.

2 ▲ Grease 8 3 in (8 cm) tartlet tins.
Roll out the pastry between 2 sheets of
greaseproof paper. Stamp out 8 4 in
(10 cm) rounds with a fluted cutter.

3 Line the tartlet tins. Prick the
bottoms. Refrigerate for 15 minutes.
Preheat a 350°F/180°C/Gas 4 oven.

4 Bake until firm, 20–25 minutes.
Cool, then remove from the tins.

5 ▲ Melt the jelly with the lemon
juice. Brush a thin layer in the bottom
of the tartlets. Whip the cream and
spread a thin layer in the tartlet cases.
Arrange the fruit on top. Brush with
the glaze and serve.

Lime Tart (top), Fruit Tartlets

Lemon Meringue Pie

SERVES 8

grated rind and juice of 1 large lemon
8 fl oz (250 ml) plus 1 tbsp cold water
4 oz (115 g) plus 6 tbsp caster sugar
1 oz (30 g) butter
3 tbsp cornflour
3 eggs, separated
⅛ tsp salt
⅛ tsp cream of tartar
FOR THE PASTRY
5 oz (140 g) plain flour
½ tsp salt
2½ oz (70 g) cold vegetable fat or lard, cut in pieces
2 tbsp iced water

1 For the pastry, sift the flour and salt into a bowl. Add the fat and cut in with a pastry blender until the mixture resembles coarse breadcrumbs. With a fork, stir in just enough water to bind the mixture. Gather the pastry into a ball.

2 ▲ On a lightly floured surface, roll out the pastry about ⅛ in (3 mm) thick. Transfer to a 9 in (23 cm) pie dish and trim the edge to leave a ½ in (2 cm) overhang.

3 ▲ Fold the overhang under and crimp the edge. Refrigerate the pastry case for at least 20 minutes.

4 Preheat a 400°F/200°C/Gas 6 oven.

5 ▲ Prick the case all over with a fork. Line with crumpled greaseproof paper and fill with baking beans. Bake for 12 minutes. Remove the paper and beans and continue baking until golden, 6–8 minutes more.

6 In a saucepan, combine the lemon rind and juice, 8 fl oz (250 ml) of the water, 4 oz (115 g) of the sugar, and butter. Bring the mixture to a boil.

7 Meanwhile, in a mixing bowl, dissolve the cornflour in the remaining water. Add the egg yolks.

> ~ **VARIATION** ~
>
> For Lime Meringue Pie, substitute the grated rind and juice of 2 medium-sized limes for the lemon.

8 ▲ Add the egg yolks to the lemon mixture and return to the boil, whisking continuously until the mixture thickens, about 5 minutes.

9 Cover the surface with greaseproof paper and let cool.

10 ▲ For the meringue, using an electric mixer beat the egg whites with the salt and cream of tartar until they hold stiff peaks. Add the remaining sugar and beat until glossy.

11 ▲ Spoon the lemon mixture into the pastry case and level. Spoon the meringue on top, smoothing it up to the pastry rim to seal. Bake until golden, 12–15 minutes.

Apple Strudel

Serves 10–12

3 oz (85 g) raisins
2 tbsp brandy
5 eating apples, such as Granny Smith or Cox's
3 large cooking apples
3½ oz (100 g) dark brown sugar
1 tsp ground cinnamon
grated rind and juice of 1 lemon
1 oz (30 g) dry breadcrumbs
2 oz (55 g) chopped pecans or walnuts
12 sheets frozen filo pastry, thawed
6 oz (170 g) butter, melted
icing sugar, for dusting

1 Soak the raisins in the brandy for at least 15 minutes.

2 ▼ Peel, core and thinly slice the apples. In a bowl, combine the sugar, cinnamon and lemon rind. Stir in the apples and half the breadcrumbs.

3 Add the raisins, nuts and lemon juice and stir until blended.

4 Preheat a 375°F/190°C/Gas 5 oven. Grease 2 baking sheets.

5 ▲ Carefully unfold the filo sheets. Keep the unused sheets covered with greaseproof paper. Lift off 1 sheet, place on a clean surface and brush with melted butter. Lay a second sheet on top and brush with butter. Continue until you have a stack of 6 buttered sheets.

6 Sprinkle a few tablespoons of breadcrumbs over the last sheet and spoon half the apple mixture at the bottom edge of the strip.

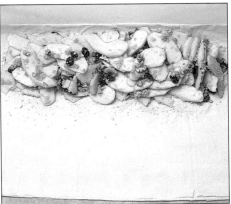

7 ▲ Starting at the apple-filled end, roll up the pastry, as for a Swiss roll. Place on a baking sheet, seam-side down, and carefully fold under the ends to seal. Repeat the procedure to make a second strudel. Brush both with butter.

8 Bake the strudels for 45 minutes. Let cool slightly. Using a small sieve, dust with a fine layer of icing sugar. Serve warm.

Treacle Tart

SERVES 4–6

6 fl oz (175 ml) golden syrup
3 oz (85 g) fresh white breadcrumbs
grated rind of 1 lemon
2 tbsp fresh lemon juice
FOR THE PASTRY
6 oz (170 g) plain flour
½ tsp salt
3 oz (85 g) cold butter, cut in pieces
1½ oz (45 g) cold margarine, cut in pieces
3–4 tbsp iced water

1 For the pastry, combine the flour and salt in a bowl. Add the butter and margarine and cut in with a pastry blender until the mixture resembles coarse breadcrumbs.

2 ▲ With a fork, stir in just enough water to bind the pastry. Gather into a ball, wrap in greaseproof paper, and refrigerate for at least 20 minutes.

3 On a lightly floured surface, roll out the pastry ⅛ in (3 mm) thick. Transfer to an 8 in (20 cm) pie dish and trim off the overhang. Refrigerate for at least 20 minutes. Reserve the trimmings for the lattice top.

4 Preheat a baking sheet at the top of a 400°F/200°C/Gas 6 oven.

5 In a saucepan, warm the syrup until thin and runny.

6 ▲ Remove from the heat and stir in the breadcrumbs and lemon rind. Let sit for 10 minutes so the bread can absorb the syrup. Add more breadcrumbs if the mixture is thin. Stir in the lemon juice and spread evenly in the pastry case.

7 Roll out the pastry trimmings and cut into 10–12 thin strips.

8 ▼ Lay half the strips on the filling, then lay the remaining strips at an angle over them to form a lattice.

9 Place on the hot sheet and bake for 10 minutes. Lower the heat to 375°F/190°C/Gas 5. Bake until golden, about 15 minutes more. Serve warm or cold.

Maple Walnut Tart

SERVES 8

3 eggs

⅛ tsp salt

2 oz (55 g) caster sugar

2 oz (55 g) butter or margarine, melted

8 fl oz (250 ml) pure maple syrup

4 oz (115 g) chopped walnuts

whipped cream, for decorating

FOR THE PASTRY

2½ oz (70 g) plain flour

2½ oz (70 g) wholewheat flour

⅛ tsp salt

2 oz (55 g) cold butter, cut in pieces

1½ oz (45 g) cold vegetable fat or lard, cut in pieces

1 egg yolk

2–3 tbsp iced water

1 ▼ For the pastry, mix the flours and salt in a bowl. Add the butter and fat and cut in with a pastry blender until the mixture resembles coarse breadcrumbs. With a fork, stir in the egg yolk and just enough water to bind the pastry. Form into a ball.

2 Wrap in greaseproof paper and refrigerate for 20 minutes.

3 Preheat a 425°F/220°C/Gas 7 oven.

4 On a lightly floured surface, roll out the pastry about ⅛ in (3 mm) thick and transfer to a 9 in (23 cm) pie dish. Trim the edge. To decorate, roll out the trimmings. With a small heart-shaped cutter, stamp out enough hearts to go around the rim of the pie. Brush the edge with water, then arrange the pastry hearts all around.

5 ▲ Prick the bottom with a fork. Line with crumpled greaseproof paper and fill with baking beans. Bake for 10 minutes. Remove the paper and beans and continue baking until golden brown, 3–6 minutes more.

6 In a bowl, whisk the eggs, salt and sugar together. Stir in the butter and maple syrup.

7 ▲ Set the pastry case on a baking sheet. Pour in the filling, then sprinkle the nuts over the top.

8 Bake until just set, about 35 minutes. Cool on a rack. Decorate with whipped cream, if wished.

Pecan Tart

SERVES 8

3 eggs
⅛ tsp salt
7 oz (200 g) dark brown sugar
4 fl oz (125 ml) golden syrup
2 tbsp fresh lemon juice
3 oz (85 g) butter, melted
5 oz (140 g) chopped pecan nuts
2 oz (55 g) pecan halves
FOR THE PASTRY
6 oz (170 g) plain flour
1 tbsp caster sugar
1 tsp baking powder
½ tsp salt
3 oz (85 g) cold unsalted butter, cut in pieces
1 egg yolk
3–4 tbsp whipping cream

1 For the pastry, sift the flour, sugar, baking powder and salt into a bowl. Add the butter and cut in with a pastry blender until the mixture resembles coarse breadcrumbs.

2 ▼ In a bowl, beat together the egg yolk and cream until blended.

~ **COOK'S TIP** ~

Serve this tart warm, accompanied by ice cream or whipped cream, if wished.

3 ▲ Pour the cream mixture into the flour mixture and stir with a fork.

4 Gather the pastry into a ball. On a lightly floured surface, roll out ⅛ in (3 mm) thick and transfer to a 9 in (23 cm) pie dish. Trim the overhang and flute the edge with your fingers. Refrigerate for at least 20 minutes.

5 Preheat a baking sheet in the middle of a 400°F/200°C/Gas 6 oven.

6 In a bowl, lightly whisk the eggs and salt. Add the sugar, syrup, lemon juice and butter. Mix well and stir in the chopped nuts.

7 ▲ Pour into the pastry case and arrange the pecan halves in concentric circles on top.

8 Bake for 10 minutes. Reduce the heat to 325°F/170°C/Gas 3; continue baking 25 minutes more.

Mince Pies

MAKES 36

6 oz (170 g) finely chopped blanched almonds

5 oz (140 g) dried apricots, finely chopped

6 oz (170 g) raisins

5 oz (140 g) currants

5 oz (140 g) glacé cherries, chopped

5 oz (140 g) cut mixed peel, chopped

4 oz (115 g) finely chopped beef suet

grated rind and juice of 2 lemons

grated rind and juice of 1 orange

7 oz (200 g) dark brown sugar

4 cooking apples, peeled, cored and chopped

2 tsp ground cinnamon

1 tsp grated nutmeg

½ tsp ground cloves

8 fl oz (250 ml) brandy

8 oz (225 g) cream cheese

2 tbsp caster sugar

icing sugar, for dusting (optional)

FOR THE PASTRY

15 oz (420 g) plain flour

5 oz (140 g) icing sugar

12 oz (350 g) cold butter, cut in pieces

grated rind and juice of 1 orange

milk, for glazing

1 Mix the nuts, dried and preserved fruit, suet, citrus rind and juice, brown sugar, apples and spices.

2 ▲ Stir in the brandy. Cover and leave in a cool place for 2 days.

3 For the pastry, sift the flour and icing sugar into a bowl. Cut in the butter until the mixture resembles coarse breadcrumbs.

4 ▲ Add the orange rind. Stir in just enough orange juice to bind. Gather into a ball, wrap in greaseproof paper, and refrigerate for at least 20 minutes.

5 Preheat a 425°F/220°C/Gas 7 oven. Grease 2–3 bun trays. Beat together the cream cheese and sugar.

6 ▲ Roll out the pastry ¼ in (5 mm) thick. With a fluted pastry cutter, stamp out 36 3 in (8 cm) rounds.

~ **COOK'S TIP** ~

The mincemeat mixture may be packed into sterilized jars and sealed. It will keep refrigerated for several months. Add a few tablespoonfuls to give apple pies a lift, or make small mincemeat-filled parcels using filo pastry.

7 ▲ Transfer the rounds to the bun tray. Fill halfway with mincemeat. Top with a teaspoonful of the cream cheese mixture.

8 ▲ Roll out the remaining pastry and stamp out 36 2 in (5 cm) rounds with a fluted cutter. Brush the edges of the pies with milk, then set the rounds on top. Cut a small steam vent in the top of each pie.

9 ▲ Brush lightly with milk. Bake until golden, 15–20 minutes. Let cool for 10 minutes before unmoulding. Dust with icing sugar, if wished.

Velvety Mocha Tart

SERVES 8

2 tsp instant espresso coffee
2 tbsp hot water
12 fl oz (350 ml) whipping cream
6 oz (170 g) plain chocolate
1 oz (30 g) bitter cooking chocolate
4 fl oz (125 ml) whipped cream, for decorating
chocolate-covered coffee beans, for decorating

FOR THE BASE

5 oz (140 g) chocolate wafers, crushed
2 tbsp caster sugar
2½ oz (70 g) butter, melted

1 ▲ For the base, mix the crushed chocolate wafers and sugar together, then stir in the melted butter.

2 Press the mixture evenly over the bottom and sides of a 9 in (23 cm) pie dish. Refrigerate until firm.

3 In a bowl, dissolve the coffee in the water and set aside.

4 Pour the cream into a mixing bowl. Set the bowl in hot water to warm the cream, bringing it closer to the temperature of the chocolate.

5 Melt both the chocolates in the top of a double boiler, or in a heatproof bowl set over a pan of hot water. Remove from the heat when nearly melted and stir to continue melting. Set the bottom of the pan in cool water to reduce the temperature. Be careful not to splash any water on the chocolate or it will become grainy.

6 ▲ With an electric mixer, whip the cream until it is lightly fluffy. Add the dissolved coffee and whip until the cream just holds its shape.

7 ▲ When the chocolate is at room temperature, fold it gently into the cream with a large metal spoon.

8 Pour into the chilled biscuit base and refrigerate until firm. To serve, pipe a ring of whipped cream rosettes around the edge, then place a chocolate-covered coffee bean in the centre of each rosette.

Coconut Cream Tart

SERVES 8

5 oz (140 g) desiccated coconut
5 oz (140 g) caster sugar
4 tbsp cornflour
⅛ tsp salt
1 pt (625 ml) milk
2 fl oz (65 ml) whipping cream
2 egg yolks
1 oz (30 g) unsalted butter
2 tsp vanilla essence
FOR THE PASTRY
5 oz (140 g) plain flour
¼ tsp salt
1½ oz (45 g) cold butter, cut in pieces
1 oz (30 g) cold vegetable fat or lard
2–3 tbsp iced water

1 For the pastry, sift the flour and salt into a bowl. Add the butter and fat and cut in with a pastry blender until the mixture resembles coarse breadcrumbs.

2 ▲ With a fork, stir in just enough water to bind the pastry. Gather into a ball, wrap in greaseproof paper and refrigerate for 20 minutes.

3 Preheat a 425°F/220°C/Gas 7 oven. Roll out the pastry ⅛ in (3 mm) thick. Line a 9 in (23 cm) pie dish. Trim and flute the edges. Prick the bottom. Line with crumpled greaseproof and fill with baking beans. Bake 10–12 minutes. Remove paper and beans, reduce heat to 350°F/180°C/Gas 4 and bake until brown, 10–15 minutes.

4 ▲ Spread 2 oz (55 g) of the coconut on a baking sheet and toast in the oven until golden, 6–8 minutes, stirring often. Set aside for decorating.

5 Put the sugar, cornflour and salt in a saucepan. In a bowl, whisk the milk, cream and egg yolks. Add the egg mixture to the saucepan.

6 ▼ Cook over a low heat, stirring, until the mixture comes to the boil. Boil for 1 minute, then remove from the heat. Add the butter, vanilla and remaining coconut.

7 Pour into the prebaked pastry case. When cool, sprinkle toasted coconut in a ring in the centre.

Chocolate Cheesecake Tart

SERVES 8

12 oz (350 g) cream cheese

4 tbsp whipping cream

8 oz (225 g) caster sugar

2 oz (55 g) cocoa powder

½ tsp ground cinnamon

3 eggs

whipped cream, for decorating

chocolate curls, for decorating

FOR THE BASE

3 oz (85 g) digestive biscuits, crushed

1½ oz (45 g) crushed amaretti biscuits (if unavailable, use extra crushed digestive biscuits)

3 oz (85 g) butter, melted

1 Preheat a baking sheet in the centre of a 350°F/180°C/Gas 4 oven.

2 For the base, mix the crushed biscuits and butter in a bowl.

3 ▲ With a spoon, press the mixture over the bottom and sides of a 9 in (23 cm) pie dish. Bake for 8 minutes. Let cool. Keep the oven on.

4 With an electric mixer, beat the cheese and cream together until smooth. Beat in the sugar, cocoa and cinnamon until blended.

5 ▼ Add the eggs, 1 at a time, beating just enough to blend.

6 Pour into the biscuit base and bake on the hot sheet for 25–30 minutes. The filling will sink down as it cools. Decorate with whipped cream and chocolate curls.

Frozen Strawberry Tart

SERVES 8

8 oz (225 g) cream cheese

8 fl oz (250 ml) soured cream

1 lb 4 oz (575 g) frozen strawberries, thawed and sliced

FOR THE BASE

4 oz (115 g) digestive biscuits, crushed

1 tbsp caster sugar

2½ oz (70 g) butter, melted

> ~ **VARIATION** ~
>
> For Frozen Raspberry Tart, use raspberries in place of the strawberries and prepare the same way, or try other frozen fruit.

1 ▲ For the base, mix together the biscuits, sugar and butter.

2 Press the mixture evenly and firmly over the bottom and sides of a 9 in (23 cm) pie dish. Freeze until firm.

3 ▼ Blend together the cream cheese and soured cream. Reserve 6 tablespoons of the strawberries. Add the rest to the cream cheese mixture.

4 Pour the filling into the biscuit base and freeze 6–8 hours until firm. To serve, spoon some of the reserved berries and juice on top.

Chocolate Cheesecake Pie (top), Frozen Strawberry Tart

CAKES & GATEAUX

~

As delicious as they are beautiful, these cakes and gâteaux are perfect to serve at teatime or for dessert. Some delightful party cakes make special occasions memorable.

Coffee-Iced Ring

SERVES 16

10 oz (285 g) plain flour

1 tbsp baking powder

1 tsp salt

12 oz (350 g) caster sugar

4 fl oz (125 ml) vegetable oil

7 eggs, at room temperature, separated

6 fl oz (175 ml) cold water

2 tsp vanilla essence

2 tsp grated lemon rind

½ tsp cream of tartar

FOR THE ICING

5½ oz (165 g) unsalted butter, at room temperature

1 lb 4 oz (575 g) icing sugar

4 tsp instant coffee dissolved in 4 tbsp hot water

1 Preheat a 325°F/170°C/Gas 3 oven.

2 ▼ Sift the flour, baking powder and salt into a bowl. Stir in 8 oz (225 g) of the sugar. Make a well in the centre and add in the following order: oil, egg yolks, water, vanilla and lemon rind. Beat with a whisk or metal spoon until smooth.

3 With an electric mixer, beat the egg whites with the cream of tartar until they hold soft peaks. Add the remaining 4 oz (115 g) of sugar and beat until they hold stiff peaks.

4 ▲ Pour the flour mixture over the whites in 3 batches, folding well after each addition.

5 Transfer the mixture to a 10 × 4 in (25 × 10 cm) ring mould and bake until the top springs back when touched lightly, about 1 hour.

6 ▲ When baked, remove from the oven and immediately hang the cake upside-down over the neck of a funnel or a narrow bottle. Let cool. To remove the cake, run a knife around the inside to loosen, then turn the tin over and tap the sides sharply. Invert the cake onto a serving plate.

7 For the icing, beat together the butter and icing sugar with an electric mixer until smooth. Add the coffee and beat until fluffy. With a metal spatula, spread over the sides and top of the cake.

Marbled Ring Cake

SERVES 16

4 oz (115 g) plain chocolate
12 oz (350 g) plain flour
1 tsp baking powder
1 lb (450 g) butter, at room temperature
1 lb 10 oz (740 g) caster sugar
1 tbsp vanilla essence
10 eggs, at room temperature
icing sugar, for dusting

1 ▲ Preheat a 350°F/180°C/Gas 4 oven. Line a 10 × 4 in (25 × 10 cm) ring mould with greaseproof paper and grease the paper. Dust with flour.

2 ▲ Melt the chocolate in the top of a double boiler, or in a heatproof bowl set over a pan of hot water. Stir occasionally. Set aside.

3 In a bowl, sift together the flour and baking powder. In another bowl, cream the butter, sugar and vanilla with an electric mixer until light and fluffy. Add the eggs, 2 at a time, then gradually incorporate the flour mixture on low speed.

4 ▲ Spoon half of the mixture into the prepared tin.

5 ▲ Stir the chocolate into the remaining mixture, then spoon into the tin. With a metal spatula, swirl the mixtures for a marbled effect.

6 Bake until a skewer inserted in the centre comes out clean, about 1 hour 45 minutes. Cover with foil halfway through baking. Let stand 15 minutes, then unmould and transfer to a cooling rack. To serve, dust with icing sugar.

Raspberry and Hazelnut Meringue Gâteau

SERVES 8

4 oz (115 g) hazelnuts

4 egg whites

⅛ tsp salt

8 oz (225 g) caster sugar

½ tsp vanilla essence

FOR THE FILLING

10 fl oz (300 ml) whipping cream

1½ lb (700 g) raspberries

1 Preheat a 350°F/180°C/Gas 4 oven. Line the bottom of 2 8 in (20 cm) cake tins with greaseproof paper and grease.

2 Spread the hazelnuts on a baking sheet and bake until lightly toasted, about 8 minutes. Let cool slightly.

3 ▲ Rub the hazelnuts vigorously in a clean tea towel to remove most of the skins.

4 Grind the nuts in a food processor, blender or grinder until they are the consistency of coarse sand.

5 Reduce heat to 300°F/150°C/Gas 2.

6 With an electric mixer, beat the egg whites and salt until they hold stiff peaks. Beat in 2 tablespoons of the sugar, then fold in the remaining sugar, a few tablespoons at a time, with a rubber spatula. Fold in the vanilla and the hazelnuts.

7 ▲ Divide the mixture between the prepared tins and spread level.

8 Bake for 1¼ hours. If the meringues brown too quickly, protect with a sheet of foil. Let stand 5 minutes, then carefully run a knife around the inside edge of the tins to loosen. Transfer to a rack to cool.

9 For the filling, whip the cream just until firm.

10 ▲ Spread half the cream in an even layer on one meringue round and top with half the raspberries.

11 Top with the other meringue round. Spread the remaining cream on top and arrange the remaining raspberries over the cream. Refrigerate for 1 hour to facilitate cutting.

Carrot Cake

SERVES 12

1 lb (450 g) carrots, peeled
6 oz (170 g) plain flour
2 tsp baking powder
½ tsp bicarbonate of soda
1 tsp salt
2 tsp ground cinnamon
4 eggs
2 tsp vanilla essence
4 oz (115 g) dark brown sugar
2 oz (55 g) caster sugar
10 fl oz (300 ml) sunflower oil
4 oz (115 g) finely chopped walnuts
3 oz (85 g) raisins
walnut halves, for decorating (optional)

FOR THE ICING

3 oz (85 g) unsalted butter, at room temperature
12 oz (350 g) icing sugar
2 fl oz (65 ml) maple syrup

1 Preheat a 350°F/180°C/Gas 4 oven. Line an 11 × 8 in (28 × 20 cm) tin with greaseproof paper and grease.

2 ▲ Grate the carrots and set aside.

3 Sift the flour, baking powder, bicarbonate of soda, salt and cinnamon into a bowl. Set aside.

4 With an electric mixer, beat the eggs until blended. Add the vanilla, sugars and oil; beat to incorporate. Add the dry ingredients, in 3 batches, folding in well after each addition.

5 ▲ Add the carrots, walnuts and raisins and fold in thoroughly.

6 Pour the mixture into the prepared tin and bake until the cake springs back when touched lightly, 40–45 minutes. Let stand 10 minutes, then unmould and transfer to a rack.

7 ▼ For the icing, cream the butter with half the icing sugar until soft. Add the syrup, then beat in the remaining sugar until blended.

8 Spread the icing over the top of the cake. Using the tip of a palette knife, make decorative ridges in the icing. Cut into squares. Decorate with walnut halves, if wished.

Plum Crumble Cake

SERVES 8–10

5 oz (140 g) butter or margarine, at room temperature

5 oz (140 g) caster sugar

4 eggs, at room temperature

1½ tsp vanilla essence

5 oz (140 g) plain flour

1 tsp baking powder

1½ lb (700 g) red plums, halved and stoned

FOR THE TOPPING

4 oz (115 g) plain flour

4½ oz (130 g) light brown sugar

1½ tsp ground cinnamon

3 oz (85 g) butter, cut in pieces

1 Preheat a 350°F/180°C/Gas 4 oven.

2 For the topping, combine the flour, light brown sugar and cinnamon in a bowl. Add the butter and work the mixture lightly with your fingertips until it resembles coarse breadcrumbs. Set aside.

3 ▲ Line a 10 × 2 in (25 × 5 cm) tin with greaseproof paper and grease.

4 Cream the butter and sugar until light and fluffy.

5 ▲ Beat in the eggs, 1 at a time. Stir in the vanilla.

6 In a bowl, sift together the flour and baking powder, then fold into the butter mixture in 3 batches.

7 ▲ Pour the mixture into the tin. Arrange the plums on top.

8 ▲ Sprinkle the topping over the plums in an even layer.

9 Bake until a skewer inserted in the centre comes out clean, about 45 minutes. Let cool in the tin.

10 To serve, run a knife around the inside edge and invert onto a plate. Invert again onto a serving plate so the topping is right-side up.

~ **VARIATION** ~

This cake can also be made with the same quantity of apricots, peeled if preferred, or stoned cherries, or use a mixture of fruit, such as red or yellow plums, greengages and apricots.

Pineapple Upside-Down Cake

SERVES 8

4 oz (115 g) butter
7 oz (200 g) dark brown sugar
16 oz (450 g) canned pineapple slices, drained
4 eggs, separated
grated rind of 1 lemon
⅛ tsp salt
4 oz (115 g) caster sugar
3 oz (85 g) plain flour
1 tsp baking powder

1 Preheat a 350°F/180°C/Gas 4 oven.

2 Melt the butter in a 10 in (25 cm) ovenproof cast-iron frying pan. Remove 1 tablespoon of the melted butter and set aside.

3 ▲ Add the brown sugar to the pan and stir until blended. Place the drained pineapple slices on top in one layer. Set aside.

~ VARIATION ~

For Dried Apricot Upside-Down Cake, replace the pineapple slices with 8 oz (225 g) of dried apricots. If they need softening, simmer the apricots in about 4 fl oz (125 ml) orange juice until plump and soft. Drain the apricots and discard any remaining cooking liquid.

---

4 In a bowl, whisk together the egg yolks, reserved butter and lemon rind until well blended. Set aside.

5 ▼ With an electric mixer, beat the egg whites with the salt until stiff. Fold in the caster sugar, 2 tablespoons at a time. Fold in the egg yolk mixture.

6 Sift the flour and baking powder together. Carefully fold into the egg mixture in 3 batches.

7 ▲ Pour the mixture over the pineapple and smooth level.

8 Bake until a skewer inserted in the centre comes out clean, about 30 minutes.

9 While still hot, place a serving plate on top of the pan, bottom-side up. Holding them tightly together with oven gloves, quickly flip over. Serve hot or cold.

Apple Ring Cake

SERVES 12

7 eating apples, such as Cox's or Granny Smith
12 fl oz (350 ml) vegetable oil
1 lb (450 g) caster sugar
3 eggs
15 oz (420 g) plain flour
1 tsp salt
1 tsp bicarbonate of soda
1 tsp ground cinnamon
1 tsp vanilla essence
4 oz (115 g) chopped walnuts
6 oz (170 g) raisins
icing sugar, for dusting

1 Preheat a 350°F/180°C/Gas 4 oven. Grease a 9 in (23 cm) ring mould.

2 ▲ Quarter, peel, core and slice the apples into a bowl. Set aside.

3 With an electric mixer, beat the oil and sugar together until blended. Add the eggs and continue beating until the mixture is creamy.

4 Sift together the flour, salt, bicarbonate of soda and cinnamon.

5 ▼ Fold the flour mixture into the egg mixture with the vanilla. Stir in the apples, walnuts and raisins.

6 Pour into the tin and bake until the cake springs back when touched lightly, about 1¼ hours. Let stand 15 minutes, then unmould and transfer to a cooling rack. Dust with a layer of icing sugar before serving.

Orange Cake

SERVES 6

6 oz (170 g) plain flour
1½ tsp baking powder
⅛ tsp salt
4 oz (115 g) butter or margarine
4 oz (115 g) caster sugar
grated rind of 1 large orange
2 eggs, at room temperature
2 tbsp milk
FOR THE SYRUP AND DECORATION
4 oz (115 g) caster sugar
8 fl oz (250 ml) fresh orange juice, strained
3 orange slices, for decorating

1 Preheat a 350°F/180°C/Gas 4 oven. Line an 8 in (20 cm) cake tin with greaseproof paper and grease the paper.

2 ▲ Sift the flour, salt and baking powder onto greaseproof paper.

3 With an electric mixer, cream the butter or margarine until soft. Add the sugar and orange rind and continue beating until light and fluffy. Beat in the eggs, 1 at a time. Fold in the flour in 3 batches, then add the milk.

4 Spoon into the tin and bake until the cake pulls away from the sides, about 30 minutes. Remove from the oven but leave in the tin.

5 Meanwhile, for the syrup, dissolve the sugar in the orange juice over a low heat. Add the orange slices and simmer for 10 minutes. Remove and drain. Let the syrup cool.

6 ▲ Prick the cake all over with a fine skewer. Pour the syrup over the hot cake. It may seem at first that there is too much syrup for the cake to absorb, but it will soak it all up. Unmould when completely cooled and decorate with small triangles of the orange slices arranged on top.

Apple Ring Cake (top), Orange Cake

Orange and Walnut Swiss Roll

SERVES 8

4 eggs, separated

4 oz (115 g) caster sugar

4 oz (115 g) very finely chopped walnuts

⅛ tsp cream of tartar

⅛ tsp salt

icing sugar, for dusting

FOR THE FILLING

10 fl oz (300 ml) whipping cream

1 tbsp caster sugar

grated rind of 1 orange

1 tbsp orange liqueur, such as Grand Marnier

1 Preheat a 350°F/180°C/Gas 4 oven. Line a 12 × 9½ in (30 × 24 cm) Swiss roll tin with greaseproof paper and grease the paper.

2 With an electric mixer, beat the egg yolks and sugar until thick.

3 ▲ Stir in the walnuts.

4 In another bowl, beat the egg whites with the cream of tartar and salt until they hold stiff peaks. Fold gently but thoroughly into the walnut mixture.

5 Pour the mixture into the prepared tin and spread level with a spatula. Bake for 15 minutes.

6 Run a knife along the inside edge to loosen, then invert the cake onto a sheet of greaseproof paper dusted with icing sugar.

7 ▲ Peel off the baking paper. Roll up the cake while it is still warm with the help of the sugared paper. Set aside to cool.

8 For the filling, whip the cream until it holds soft peaks. Stir together the caster sugar and orange rind, then fold into the whipped cream. Add the liqueur.

9 ▲ Gently unroll the cake. Spread the inside with a layer of orange whipped cream, then re-roll. Keep refrigerated until ready to serve. Dust the top with icing sugar just before serving.

Chocolate Swiss Roll

SERVES 10

8 oz (225 g) plain chocolate
3 tbsp water
2 tbsp rum, brandy or strong coffee
7 eggs, separated
6 oz (170 g) caster sugar
⅛ tsp salt
12 fl oz (350 ml) whipping cream
icing sugar, for dusting

1 Preheat a 350°F/180°C/Gas 4 oven. Line a 15 × 13 in (38 × 33 cm) Swiss roll tin with greaseproof paper and grease the paper.

2 ▲ Combine the chocolate, water and rum or other flavouring in the top of a double boiler, or in a heatproof bowl set over hot water. Heat until melted. Set aside.

3 With an electric mixer, beat the egg yolks and sugar until thick.

4 ▲ Stir in the melted chocolate.

5 In another bowl, beat the egg whites and salt until they hold stiff peaks. Fold a large dollop of egg whites into the yolk mixture to lighten it, then carefully fold in the rest of the whites.

6 ▼ Pour the mixture into the pan; smooth evenly with a metal spatula.

7 Bake for 15 minutes. Remove from the oven, cover with greaseproof paper and a damp cloth. Let stand for 1–2 hours.

8 With an electric mixer, whip the cream until stiff. Set aside.

9 Run a knife along the inside edge to loosen, then invert the cake onto a sheet of greaseproof paper that has been dusted with icing sugar.

10 Peel off the baking paper. Spread with an even layer of whipped cream, then roll up the cake with the help of the sugared paper.

11 Refrigerate for several hours. Before serving, dust with an even layer of icing sugar.

Best-Ever Chocolate Sandwich

SERVES 12–14

4 oz (115 g) unsalted butter
4 oz (115 g) plain flour
2 oz (55 g) cocoa powder
1 tsp baking powder
⅛ tsp salt
6 eggs
8 oz (225 g) caster sugar
2 tsp vanilla essence
FOR THE ICING
8 oz (225 g) plain chocolate, chopped
3 oz (85 g) unsalted butter
3 eggs, separated
8 fl oz (250 ml) whipping cream
3 tbsp caster sugar

1 Preheat a 350°F/180°C/Gas 4 oven. Line 3 8 × 1½ in (20 × 3 cm) round tins with greaseproof paper and grease.

2 ▲ Dust evenly with flour and spread with a brush. Set aside.

~ VARIATION ~

For a simpler icing, combine 8 fl oz (250 ml) whipping cream with 8 oz (225 g) finely chopped plain chocolate in a saucepan. Stir over a low heat until the chocolate has melted. Cool and whisk to spreading consistency.

3 ▲ Melt the butter over a low heat. With a spoon, skim off any foam that rises to the surface. Set aside.

4 ▲ Sift the flour, cocoa, baking powder and salt together 3 times and set aside.

5 Place the eggs and sugar in a large heatproof bowl set over a pan of hot water. With an electric mixer, beat until the mixture doubles in volume and is thick enough to leave a ribbon trail when the beaters are lifted, about 10 minutes. Add the vanilla.

6 ▲ Sift over the dry ingredients in 3 batches, folding in carefully after each addition. Fold in the butter.

7 Divide the mixture between the tins and bake until the cakes pull away from the sides of the tin, about 25 minutes. Transfer to a rack.

8 For the icing, melt the chopped chocolate in the top of a double boiler, or in a heatproof bowl set over hot water.

9 ▲ Off the heat, stir in the butter and egg yolks. Return to a low heat and stir until thick. Remove from the heat and set aside.

10 Whip the cream until firm; set aside. In another bowl, beat the egg whites until stiff. Add the sugar and beat until glossy.

11 Fold the cream into the chocolate mixture, then carefully fold in the egg whites. Refrigerate for 20 minutes to thicken the icing.

12 ▲ Sandwich the cake layers with icing, stacking them carefully. Spread the remaining icing evenly over the top and sides of the cake.

Rich Chocolate Nut Cake

SERVES 10

8 oz (225 g) butter
8 oz (225 g) plain chocolate
4 oz (115 g) cocoa powder
12 oz (350 g) caster sugar
6 eggs
3 fl oz (85 ml) brandy or cognac
8 oz (225 g) finely chopped hazelnuts
FOR THE GLAZE
2 oz (55 g) butter
5 oz (140 g) bitter cooking chocolate
2 tbsp milk
1 tsp vanilla essence

1 Preheat a 350°F/180°C/Gas 4 oven. Line a 9 × 2 in (23 × 5 cm) round tin with greaseproof paper and grease.

2 Melt the butter and chocolate together in the top of a double boiler, or in a heatproof bowl set over hot water. Set aside to cool.

3 ▼ Sift the cocoa into a bowl. Add the sugar and eggs and stir until just combined. Pour in the melted chocolate mixture and brandy.

4 Fold in three-quarters of the nuts, then pour the mixture into the prepared tin.

5 ▲ Set the tin inside a large tin and pour 1 in (2.5 cm) of hot water into the outer tin. Bake until the cake is firm to the touch, about 45 minutes. Let stand 15 minutes, then unmould and transfer to a cooling rack.

6 Wrap the cake in greaseproof paper and refrigerate for 6 hours.

7 For the glaze, combine the butter, chocolate, milk and vanilla in the top of a double boiler or in a heatproof bowl set over hot water, until melted.

8 Place a piece of greaseproof paper under the cake, then drizzle spoonfuls of glaze along the edge to drip down and coat the sides. Pour the remaining glaze on top of the cake.

9 ▲ Cover the sides of the cake with the remaining nuts, gently pressing them on with the palm of your hand.

Chocolate Layer Cake

SERVES 8–10

4 oz (115 g) plain chocolate
6 oz (170 g) butter
1 lb (450 g) caster sugar
3 eggs
1 tsp vanilla essence
6 oz (170 g) plain flour
1 tsp baking powder
4 oz (115 g) chopped walnuts
FOR THE TOPPING
12 fl oz (350 ml) whipping cream
8 oz (225 g) plain chocolate
1 tbsp vegetable oil

1 Preheat a 350°F/180°C/Gas 4 oven. Line 2 8 in (20 cm) cake tins with greaseproof paper and grease.

2 Melt the chocolate and butter together in the top of a double boiler, or in a heatproof bowl set over a saucepan of hot water.

3 ▲ Transfer to a mixing bowl and stir in the sugar. Add the eggs and vanilla and mix until well blended.

~ VARIATION ~

To make Chocolate Ice Cream Layer Cake, sandwich the cake layers with softened vanilla ice cream. Freeze before serving.

4 ▲ Sift over the flour and baking powder. Stir in the walnuts.

5 Divide the mixture between the prepared tins and spread level.

6 Bake until a skewer inserted in the centre comes out clean, about 30 minutes. Let stand 10 minutes, then unmould and transfer to a rack.

7 When the cakes are cool, whip the cream until firm. With a long serrated knife, carefully slice each cake in half horizontally.

8 Sandwich the layers with some of the whipped cream and spread the remainder over the top and sides of the cake. Refrigerate until needed.

9 ▼ For the chocolate curls, melt the chocolate and oil in the top of a double boiler or a bowl set over hot water. Transfer to a non-porous surface. Spread to a ⅜ in (1 cm) thick rectangle. Just before the chocolate sets, hold the blade of a straight knife at an angle to the chocolate and scrape across the surface to make curls. Place on top of the cake.

Nut and Apple Gâteau

SERVES 8

4 oz (115 g) pecan nuts or walnuts

2 oz (55 g) plain flour

2 tsp baking powder

¼ tsp salt

2 large cooking apples

3 eggs

8 oz (225 g) caster sugar

1 tsp vanilla essence

6 fl oz (175 ml) whipping cream

1 Preheat a 325°F/170°C/Gas 3 oven. Line 2 9 in (23 cm) cake tins with greaseproof paper and grease the paper. Spread the nuts on a baking sheet and bake for 10 minutes.

2 Finely chop the nuts. Reserve 1½ tablespoons and place the rest in a mixing bowl. Sift over the flour, baking powder and salt and stir.

3 ▲ Quarter, core and peel the apples. Cut into ⅛ in (3 mm) dice, then stir into the nut-flour mixture.

4 ▲ With an electric mixer, beat the eggs until frothy. Gradually add the sugar and vanilla and beat until a ribbon forms, about 8 minutes. Gently fold in the flour mixture.

5 Pour into the tins and level the tops. Bake until a skewer inserted in the centre comes out clean, about 35 minutes. Let stand 10 minutes.

6 ▲ To loosen, run a knife around the inside edge of each layer. Let cool.

7 ▲ Whip the cream until firm. Spread half over the cake. Top with the second cake. Pipe whipped cream rosettes on top and sprinkle over the reserved nuts before serving.

Almond Cake

SERVES 4–6

8 oz (225 g) blanched whole almonds, plus more for decorating
1 oz (30 g) butter
3 oz (85 g) icing sugar
3 eggs
½ tsp almond essence
1 oz (30 g) plain flour
3 egg whites
1 tbsp caster sugar

1 ▲ Preheat a 325°F/170°C/Gas 3 oven. Line a 9 in (23 cm) round cake tin with greaseproof paper and grease.

2 ▲ Spread the almonds in a baking tray and toast for 10 minutes. Cool, then coarsely chop 8 oz (225 g).

3 Melt the butter and set aside.

4 Preheat a 400°F/200°C/Gas 6 oven.

5 Grind the chopped almonds with half the icing sugar in a food processor, blender or grinder. Transfer to a mixing bowl.

6 ▲ Add the whole eggs and remaining icing sugar. With an electric mixer, beat until the mixture forms a ribbon when the beaters are lifted. Mix in the butter and almond essence. Sift over the flour and fold in gently.

7 With an electric mixer, beat the egg whites until they hold soft peaks. Add the caster sugar and beat until stiff and glossy.

8 ▲ Fold the whites into the almond mixture in 4 batches.

9 Spoon the mixture into the prepared tin and bake in the centre of the oven until golden brown, about 15–20 minutes. Decorate the top with the remaining toasted whole almonds. Serve warm.

Light Fruit Cake

Makes 2 loaves

8 oz (225 g) prunes
8 oz (225 g) dates
8 oz (225 g) currants
8 oz (225 g) sultanas
8 fl oz (250 ml) dry white wine
8 fl oz (250 ml) rum
12 oz (350 g) plain flour
2 tsp baking powder
1 tsp ground cinnamon
½ tsp grated nutmeg
8 oz (225 g) butter, at room temperature
8 oz (225 g) caster sugar
4 eggs, at room temperature, lightly beaten
1 tsp vanilla essence

1 Stone the prunes and dates and chop finely. Place in a bowl with the currants and sultanas.

2 ▲ Stir in the wine and rum and let stand, covered, for 48 hours. Stir occasionally.

3 Preheat a 300°F/150°C/Gas 2 oven with a tray of hot water in the bottom. Line 2 9 × 5 in (23 × 13 cm) tins with greaseproof paper and grease.

4 Sift together the flour, baking powder, cinnamon, and nutmeg.

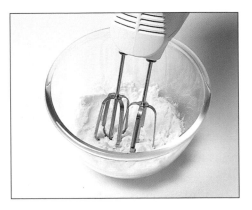

5 ▲ With an electric mixer, cream the butter and sugar together until light and fluffy.

6 Gradually add the eggs and vanilla. Fold in the flour mixture in 3 batches. Fold in the dried fruit mixture and its soaking liquid.

7 ▲ Divide the mixture between the tins and bake until a skewer inserted in the centre comes out clean, about 1½ hours.

8 Let stand 20 minutes, then unmould and transfer to a cooling rack. Wrap in foil and store in an airtight container. If possible, leave for at least 1 week before serving to allow the flavours to mellow.

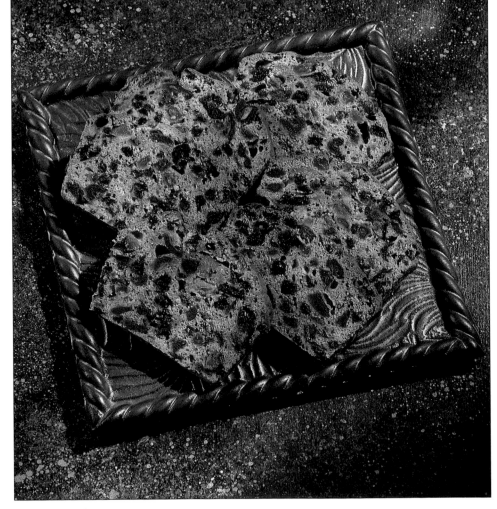

Rich Fruit Cake

SERVES 12

5 oz (140 g) currants

6 oz (170 g) raisins

2 oz (55 g) sultanas

2 oz (55 g) glacé cherries, halved

3 tbsp sweet sherry

6 oz (170 g) butter

7 oz (200 g) dark brown sugar

2 size 1 eggs, at room temperature

7 oz (200 g) plain flour

2 tsp baking powder

2 tsp each ground ginger, allspice, and cinnamon

1 tbsp golden syrup

1 tbsp milk

2 oz (55 g) cut mixed peel

4 oz (115 g) chopped walnuts

FOR THE DECORATION

8 oz (225 g) caster sugar

4 fl oz (125 ml) water

1 lemon, thinly sliced

½ orange, thinly sliced

4 fl oz (125 ml) orange marmalade

glacé cherries

1 One day before preparing, combine the currants, raisins, sultanas and cherries in a bowl. Stir in the sherry. Cover and let stand overnight to soak.

2 Preheat a 300°F/150°C/Gas 2 oven. Line a 9 × 3 in (23 × 8 cm) springform tin with greaseproof paper and grease. Place a tray of hot water on the bottom of the oven.

3 With an electric mixer, cream the butter and sugar until light and fluffy. Beat in the eggs, 1 at a time.

4 ▲ Sift the flour, baking powder and spices together 3 times. Fold into the butter mixture in 3 batches. Fold in the syrup, milk, dried fruit and liquid, mixed peel and nuts.

5 ▲ Spoon into the tin, spreading out so there is a slight depression in the centre of the mixture.

6 Bake until a skewer inserted in the centre comes out clean, 2½–3 hours. Cover with foil when the top is golden to prevent over-browning. Cool in the tin on a rack.

7 ▲ For the decoration, combine the sugar and water in a saucepan and bring to the boil. Add the lemon and orange slices and cook until crystallized, about 20 minutes. Work in batches, if necessary. Remove the fruit with a slotted spoon. Pour the remaining syrup over the cake and let cool. Melt the marmalade over low heat, then brush over the top of the cake. Decorate with the crystallized citrus slices and cherries.

Whiskey Cake

MAKES 1 LOAF

6 oz (170 g) chopped walnuts

3 oz (85 g) raisins, chopped

3 oz (85 g) currants

4 oz (115 g) plain flour

1 tsp baking powder

¼ tsp salt

4 oz (115 g) butter

8 oz (225 g) caster sugar

3 eggs, at room temperature, separated

1 tsp grated nutmeg

½ tsp ground cinnamon

3 fl oz (85 ml) Irish whiskey or bourbon

icing sugar, for dusting

1 ▼ Preheat a 325°F/170°C/Gas 3 oven. Line a 9 × 5 in (23 × 13 cm) loaf tin with greaseproof paper. Grease the paper and sides of the pan.

2 ▲ Place the walnuts, raisins, and currants in a bowl. Sprinkle over 2 tablespoons of the flour, mix and set aside. Sift together the remaining flour, baking powder and salt.

3 ▲ Cream the butter and sugar until light and fluffy. Beat in the egg yolks.

4 Mix the nutmeg, cinnamon and whiskey. Fold into the butter mixture, alternating with the flour mixture.

5 ▲ In another bowl, beat the egg whites until stiff. Fold into the whiskey mixture until just blended. Fold in the walnut mixture.

6 Bake until a skewer inserted in the centre comes out clean, about 1 hour. Let cool in the pan. Dust with icing sugar over a template.

Gingerbread

SERVES 8–10

1 tbsp vinegar
6 fl oz (175 ml) milk
6 oz (170 g) plain flour
2 tsp baking powder
¼ tsp bicarbonate of soda
½ tsp salt
2 tsp ground ginger
1 tsp ground cinnamon
¼ tsp ground cloves
4 oz (115 g) butter, at room temperature
4 oz (115 g) caster sugar
1 egg, at room temperature
6 fl oz (175 ml) black treacle
whipped cream, for serving
chopped stem ginger, for decorating

1 ▲ Preheat a 350°F/180°C/Gas 4 oven. Line an 8 in (20 cm) square cake tin with greaseproof paper and grease the paper and the sides of the pan.

2 ▲ Add the vinegar to the milk and set aside. It will curdle.

3 In another mixing bowl, sift all the dry ingredients together 3 times and set aside.

4 With an electric mixer, cream the butter and sugar until light and fluffy. Beat in the egg until well combined.

5 ▼ Stir in the black treacle.

6 ▲ Fold in the dry ingredients in 4 batches, alternating with the curdled milk. Mix only enough to blend.

7 Pour into the prepared tin and bake until firm, 45–50 minutes. Cut into squares and serve warm, with whipped cream. Decorate with the stem ginger.

Heart Cake

MAKES 1 CAKE

8 oz (225 g) butter or margarine, at room temperature

8 oz (225 g) caster sugar

4 eggs, at room temperature

6 oz (170 g) plain flour

1 tsp baking powder

½ tsp bicarbonate of soda

2 tbsp milk

1 tsp vanilla essence

FOR ICING AND DECORATING

3 egg whites

12 oz (350 g) caster sugar

2 tbsp cold water

2 tbsp fresh lemon juice

¼ tsp cream of tartar

pink food colouring

3–4 oz (85–115 g) icing sugar

1 Preheat a 350°F/180°C/Gas 4 oven. Line an 8 in (20 cm) heart-shaped tin with greaseproof paper and grease.

2 ▲ With an electric mixer, cream the butter or margarine and sugar until light and fluffy. Add the eggs, 1 at a time, beating thoroughly after each addition.

3 Sift the flour, baking powder and baking soda together. Fold the dry ingredients into the butter mixture in 3 batches, alternating with the milk. Stir in the vanilla.

4 ▲ Spoon the mixture into the prepared tin and bake until a skewer inserted in the centre comes out clean, 35–40 minutes. Let the cake stand in the tin for 5 minutes, then unmould and transfer to a rack to cool completely.

5 For the icing, combine 2 of the egg whites, the caster sugar, water, lemon juice and cream of tartar in the top of a double boiler or in a bowl set over simmering water. With an electric mixer, beat until thick and holding soft peaks, about 7 minutes. Remove from the heat and continue beating until the mixture is thick enough to spread. Tint the icing with the pink food colouring.

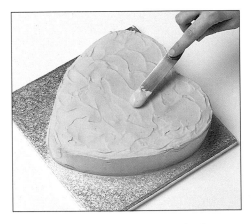

6 ▲ Put the cake on a board, about 12 in (30 cm) square, covered in foil or in paper suitable for contact with food. Spread the icing evenly on the cake. Smooth the top and sides. Leave to set for 3–4 hours, or overnight.

7 ▲ For the paper piping bags, fold an 11 × 8 in (28 × 20 cm) sheet of greaseproof paper in half diagonally, then cut into 2 pieces along the fold mark. Roll over the short side, so that it meets the right-angled corner and forms a cone. To form the piping bag, hold the cone in place with one hand, wrap the point of the long side of the triangle around the cone, and tuck inside, folding over twice to secure. Snip a hole in the pointed end and slip in a small metal piping nozzle to extend about ¼ in (5 mm).

8 For the piped decorations, place 1 tablespoon of the remaining egg white in a bowl and whisk until frothy. Gradually beat in enough icing sugar to make a stiff mixture suitable for piping.

9 ▲ Spoon into a paper piping bag to half-fill. Fold over the top and squeeze to pipe decorations on the top and sides of the cake.

Iced Fancies

MAKES 16

4 oz (115 g) butter, at room temperature

8 oz (225 g) caster sugar

2 eggs, at room temperature

6 oz (170 g) plain flour

¼ tsp salt

1½ tsp baking powder

4 fl oz (125 ml) plus 1 tbsp milk

1 tsp vanilla essence

FOR ICING AND DECORATING

2 large egg whites

14 oz (400 g) sifted icing sugar

1–2 drops glycerine

juice of 1 lemon

food colourings

hundreds and thousands, for decorating

crystallized lemon and orange slices, for decorating

1 Preheat a 375°F/190°C/Gas 5 oven.

2 ▲ Line 16 bun-tray cups with fluted paper baking cases, or grease.

~ COOK'S TIP ~

Ready-made cake decorating products are widely available, and may be used, if preferred, instead of the recipes given for icing and decorating. Coloured icing in ready-to-pipe tubes is useful.

3 With an electric mixer, cream the butter and sugar until light and fluffy. Add the eggs, 1 at a time, beating well after each addition.

4 Sift together the flour, salt and baking powder. Stir into the butter mixture, alternating with the milk. Stir in the vanilla.

5 ▲ Fill the cups half-full and bake until the tops spring back when touched lightly, about 20 minutes. Let the cakes stand in the tray for 5 minutes, then unmould and transfer to a rack to cool completely.

6 For the icing, beat the egg whites until stiff but not dry. Gradually add the sugar, glycerine and lemon juice, and continue beating for 1 minute. The consistency should be spreadable. If necessary, thin with a little water or add more sifted icing sugar.

7 ▲ Divide the icing between several bowls and tint with food colourings. Spread different coloured icings over the cooled cakes.

8 ▲ Decorate the cakes as wished, with sugar decorations such as hundreds and thousands.

9 ▲ Other decorations include crystallized orange and lemon slices. Cut into small pieces and arrange on top of the cakes. Alternatively, use other suitable sweets.

10 ▲ To make freehand iced decorations, fill paper piping bags (see page 118) with different colour icings. Pipe on faces, or make other designs.

Sun Cake

SERVES 10–12

4 oz (115 g) unsalted butter
6 eggs
8 oz (225 g) caster sugar
4 oz (115 g) plain flour
½ tsp salt
1 tsp vanilla essence
FOR ICING AND DECORATING
1 oz (30 g) unsalted butter, at room temperature
1 lb (450 g) sifted icing sugar
4 fl oz (125 ml) apricot jam
2 tbsp water
2 large egg whites
1–2 drops glycerine
juice of 1 lemon
yellow and orange food colourings

1 Preheat a 350°F/180°C/Gas 4 oven. Line 2 8 × 2 in (20 × 5 cm) round cake tins, then grease and flour.

2 In a saucepan, melt the butter over very low heat. Skim off any foam that rises to the surface, then set aside.

3 ▲ Place a heatproof bowl over a saucepan of hot water. Add the eggs and sugar. Beat with an electric mixer until the mixture doubles in volume and is thick enough to leave a ribbon trail when the beaters are lifted, 8–10 minutes.

4 Sift the flour and salt together 3 times. Sift over the egg mixture in 3 batches, folding in well after each addition. Fold in the melted butter and vanilla.

5 Divide the mixture between the tins. Level the surfaces and bake until the cakes shrink slightly from the sides of the tins, 25–30 minutes. Let stand 5 minutes, then unmould and transfer to a cooling rack.

6 Prepare a board, 16 in (40 cm) square, covered in paper suitable for contact with food, or in foil.

7 ▲ For the sunbeams, cut one of the cakes into 8 equal wedges. Cut away a rounded piece from the base of each so that they fit neatly up against the sides of the whole cake.

8 ▲ For the butter icing, mix the butter and 1 oz (30 g) of the icing sugar. Use to attach the sunbeams.

9 ▲ Melt the jam with the water and brush over the cake. Place on the board and straighten, if necessary.

10 ▲ For the icing, beat the egg whites until stiff but not dry. Gradually add 14 oz (400 g) icing sugar, the glycerine and lemon juice, and continue beating for 1 minute. If necessary, thin with water or add a little more sugar. Tint with yellow food colouring and spread over the cake.

11 ▲ Divide the remaining icing in half and tint with more food colouring to obtain bright yellow and orange. Pipe decorative zigzags on the sunbeams and a face in the middle.

Classic Cheesecake

SERVES 8

2 oz (55 g) digestive biscuits, crushed

2 lb (900 g) cream cheese, at room temperature

10 oz (285 g) caster sugar

grated rind of 1 lemon

3 tbsp fresh lemon juice

1 tsp vanilla essence

4 eggs, at room temperature

1 Preheat a 325°F/170°C/Gas 3 oven. Grease an 8 in (20 cm) springform tin. Place on a round of foil about 4 in (10 cm) larger than the diameter of the tin. Press it up the sides to seal tightly.

2 Sprinkle the biscuit crumbs in the base of the tin. Press to form an even layer.

3 With an electric mixer, beat the cream cheese until smooth. Add the sugar, lemon rind and juice and vanilla, and beat until blended. Beat in the eggs, 1 at a time. Beat just enough to blend thoroughly.

4 ▲ Pour into the prepared tin. Set the tin in a larger baking tin and place in the oven. Pour enough hot water in the outer tin to come 1 in (2.5 cm) up the side of the tin.

5 Bake until the top of the cake is golden brown, about 1½ hours. Let cool in the tin.

6 ▼ Run a knife around the edge to loosen, then remove the rim of the tin. Refrigerate for at least 4 hours before serving.

Chocolate Cheesecake

SERVES 10–12

6 oz (170 g) plain chocolate

4 oz (115 g) bitter cooking chocolate

2½ lb (1.2 kg) cream cheese, at room temperature

8 oz (225 g) caster sugar

2 tsp vanilla essence

4 eggs, at room temperature

6 fl oz (175 ml) soured cream

FOR THE BASE

5 oz (140 g) chocolate wafers, crushed

3 oz (85 g) butter, melted

½ tsp ground cinnamon

1 Preheat a 350°F/180°C/Gas 4 oven. Grease the bottom and sides of a 9 × 3 in (23 × 8 cm) springform tin.

2 ▲ For the base, mix the crushed chocolate wafers with the butter and cinnamon. Press evenly in the bottom of the tin.

3 Melt both chocolates in the top of a double boiler, or in a heatproof bowl set over hot water. Set aside.

4 With an electric mixer, beat the cream cheese until smooth, then beat in the sugar and vanilla. Add the eggs, 1 at a time, scraping the bowl with a spatula when necessary.

5 Add the soured cream. Stir in the melted chocolate.

6 ▼ Pour over the base. Bake for 1 hour. Let cool in the tin; remove the rim. Refrigerate before serving.

Classic Cheesecake (top), Chocolate Cheesecake

Lemon Mousse Cheesecake

SERVES 10–12

2½ lb (1.2 kg) cream cheese, at room temperature

12 oz (350 g) caster sugar

1½ oz (45 g) plain flour

4 eggs, at room temperature, separated

4 fl oz (125 ml) fresh lemon juice

grated rind of 2 lemons

4 oz (115 g) digestive biscuits, crushed

1 Preheat a 325°F/170°C/Gas 3 oven. Line a 10 × 2 in (25 × 5 cm) round cake tin with greaseproof paper and grease the paper.

2 With an electric mixer, beat the cream cheese until smooth. Gradually add 10 oz (285 g) of the sugar, and beat until light. Beat in the flour.

3 ▲ Add the egg yolks, and lemon juice and rind, and beat until smooth and well blended.

4 In another bowl, beat the egg whites until they hold soft peaks. Add the remaining sugar and beat until stiff and glossy.

5 ▲ Add the egg whites to the cheese mixture and gently fold in.

6 Pour the mixture into the prepared tin, then place the tin in a larger baking tin. Place in the oven and pour hot water in the outer tin to come 1 in (2.5 cm) up the side.

7 Bake until golden, 60–65 minutes. Let cool in the pan on a rack. Cover and refrigerate for at least 4 hours.

8 To unmould, run a knife around the inside edge. Place a flat plate, bottom-side up, over the pan and invert onto the plate. Smooth the top with a metal spatula.

9 ▲ Sprinkle the biscuits over the top in an even layer, pressing down slightly to make a top crust.

10 To serve, cut slices with a sharp knife dipped in hot water.

Index

~